no animals
were harmed
in the
mAKing of
this booK !

An Hour On Sunday

creating moments of transformation and wonder

NANCY BEACH

WILLOW
Willow Creek Resources

ZONDERVAN™

GRAND RAPIDS, MICHIGAN 49530 USA

An Hour On Sunday

COPYRIGHT 2004 BY NANCY BEACH

Requests for information should be addressed to:
Zondervan, *Grand Rapids, Michigan 49530*

Library of Congress Cataloging-in-Publication Data

Beach, Nancy.
An hour on Sunday: creating moments of transformation
and wonder / Nancy Beach ; illustrated by Travis King and
Kathee Biaggne; photography by Steve Sonheim and
Kathee Biaggne.
    p. cm.
"Willow Creek Resources."
ISBN 0-310-25296-2
1. Public worship. 2. Church. I. Title.
BV15.B42 2004
264—dc22

2003018785

This edition printed on acid-free paper.

Interior and cover design by Kathee Biaggne.
Illustrations by Travis King and Kathee Biaggne.
Photography by Steve Sonheim and Kathee Biaggne.

Printed in the United States of America

04 05 06 07 08 09/ BTP /10 9 8 7 6 5 4 3

copyright info

CASt (in order of appearance)

PArt ONE: GETTING READY FOR SUNDAYS

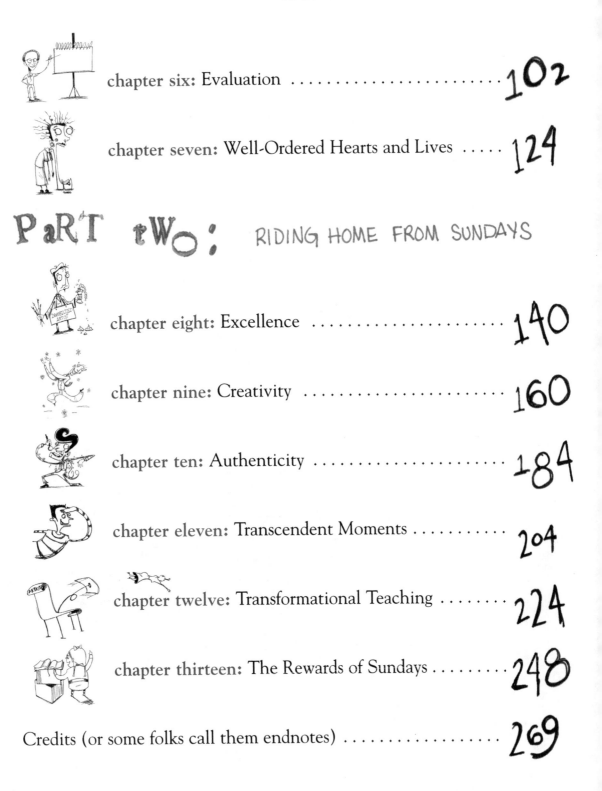

ForeWOrD

Picture a twenty-two-year-old guy, his wounds still raw from leaving a promising family business. He nervously paces with some scribbled message notes and a Bible in a church sanctuary that, in thirty minutes, will be packed with high school students. He has given a grand total of five talks in his life.

In walks an energetic, high school sophomore with a friend. She asks me what I am going to teach that night. I stumble through the gist of it and notice her creative gears beginning to turn. "What if we put a little drama together before you give your talk?"

Drama? I think to myself. *Wouldn't that require a script? Wouldn't the script need actors? And wouldn't the actors need rehearsals? The doors open in twenty-eight minutes!* But the leader in me could tell this was not your average high school sophomore. The drama idea wasn't motivated by a self-seeking need to be in the spotlight. The motivation came from a genuine desire for her peers to experience God's love and power in more ways than just the spoken word. Her proposal was not made on a whim. On the contrary, she knew what was at stake and how focused she and others would have to be to pull it off. How could I say no?

When I am long gone and forgotten, those who reflect on church history will still be writing about unleashing the arts in the local church in the latter part of the twentieth century. How did it ever become normal to use contemporary Christian music, drama, dance, and electronic media in the local church? How did bench-sitting artists wind up as key players in the redemptive drama of the church? How did "programming departments" get created in thousands of churches all over the world? And how did it become normal for women and men to sit together on senior leadership teams and partner with pastors to make church services come alive?

Honest historians will have to give a lot of ink to Nancy Beach. For over thirty years she has relentlessly sought to communicate the message of the Christian faith through art forms that cause seekers and believers alike to stop dead in their tracks and say, "Whoa! That was a God moment! Now what must I do?"

Nancy's amazing accomplishments flow out of an unshakable conviction that the local church is the hope of the world and that, unless and until all artists in the church get into the game, the church will never reach its redemptive potential. Her ministry at Willow Creek Community Church has resulted in hundreds of artists using their gifts for God. Her ministry through the Willow Creek Association has touched tens of thousands of artists all around the world.

On a personal note, Nancy has been a friend for more than three decades. I watched her graduate from high school, college, and graduate school. I watched her walk the wedding aisle and dedicate her children to God. We have seen each other at our respective "worsts." Hard words have been said both ways, dozens of apologies have been offered to one another after difficult programs. I have watched more than a few of her creative ideas go down in flames, and she has sat through more than her share of my messages that never took off. And yet, I would go into any kingdom battle with Nancy, any time. She loves God, loves the church, loves people, and plays to win for the glory of the One whose name she has pointed the world to her entire adult life. She is the real deal and her writing bears that out. Anyone can write theory. These days most writing about the arts in church is penned by those who observe from afar. Only a few can distill decades of weekly ministry warfare into a book that will inspire artists now and for generations to come.

> 66 . . . unless and until all artists in the church get into the game, the church will never reach its redemptive potential. 99

If you are an artist or arts ministry leader, my prayer is that you will discover you are not alone in the struggle to use your gifts in the church. Don't give up on your calling. I can't imagine the local church or God's kingdom without you. If you lead a team, I encourage you to read and wrestle together to apply the values this book describes.

If you are a pastor, don't just pass this book along to your music minister or drama director. Effective use of the arts in church requires partnership and mutual respect. Pastors, especially, need to move from tolerating artists to treasuring them. The most effective services are those we craft together, skillfully and lovingly.

—**Bill Hybels, founding and senior pastor, Willow Creek Community Church**

gRaTiTuDeS
(aka THANK YOU, THANK YOU!)

My life's path has been shaped and inspired by so many others. I am deeply grateful to my parents, Warren and Peggy Moore, for blessing me with an early introduction to Jesus and a devotion to the local church. Teachers and writers stretched my mind and awakened my heart, including Don Martello, Hal Chastain, Em Griffin, Jim Young, Philip Yancey, Madeleine L'Engle, Ken Gire, Frederick Buechner, and John Ortberg.

I owe a tremendous debt of gratitude to my earliest mentors in ministry, Bill Hybels and the late Dave Holmbo. Their insights, vision, and values leap out of every page.

This book would not have been written without the prodding and support of Bruce Smith, Joe Sherman, and Doug Veenstra. My dear friends and fellow writers Jane Stephens and Caron Loveless read every chapter and offered truthful, loving feedback that made each one stronger. I was surrounded by a skilled publishing team including Nancy Raney, Mark Kemink, and Doug Yonamine from the Willow Creek Association and John Raymond and Alicia Mey from Zondervan. Christine Anderson pored over every sentence, giving me the confidence I required to send it on to Jack Kuhatschek, a wonderfully encouraging and perceptive editor for this rookie writer. Copy editor Joan Huyser-Honig helped me communicate with far fewer words. I am also grateful for the daily support and encouragement of my assistant, Ann Keefer, who enables me to do life and ministry more sanely.

From my first encounter with art director Kathee Biaggne, I knew I had found a rare individual with huge vision, childlike imagination, and a remarkable work ethic. She made this book look and feel so much better than I dreamed, and the process of collaborating with her was truly a blast. Many thanks as well to illustrator Travis King and photographer Steve Sonheim for their delightful contributions.

Rich and Karen, thank you for graciously refilling my teacup as I wrote from a corner at Caribou Coffee. I deeply appreciate the loving support of my movie buddies and tremendous friends, Lynn and Karla.

I am indebted every day of my ministry to the artists of Willow Creek Community Church. They inspire me with their fierce devotion to Christ and their local church and their tremendous sacrifices of time, energy, and passion. I owe a special thank-you to long-time team members and treasured friends, including Rory, Steve, Greg, Corinne, Pam, Tom, Bruce, Mark, Joe, Larry, and Lori. I receive far too much credit for their creative genius. If I'm at all like Jesus, it is largely because of their ruthless love for me. I hope God allows us to do ministry together until our final days on earth.

Finally, there are three faces I most cherish, three people who remind me I am loved not for what I do but, at least in their eyes, for just being me. Warren, Samantha, and Johanna—it is a gift beyond words to be a member of our little family. Thank you for freeing me to pursue my calling and for putting up with too many take-out meals and a not-so-present mom for a few months. (I love you more than you love me, one-two-three no change-backs.) I can't wait to see the ways God will use my girls to communicate to their generation in the hours on Sunday.

"Warren, Samantha, and Johanna—it is a gift beyond words to be a member of our little family."

Nancy

Getting Ready for Sundays

Before any hour on Sunday is created and experienced, an arts ministry needs to establish some foundational values. While these values may not be viewed as the "fun" part, they are absolutely essential and require our full attention, devotion, thinking, and, ultimately, action. Resist the temptation to move too quickly through part one—we ignore these values to our peril.

chapter **one**

The hour
on Sunday
can be
a time of
wonder, a
time of
transformation,
maybe even
a time
of awe.

The Wonder
of Sundays

9:23 A.M. Sunday morning. A young mother shouts upstairs to see if her five-year-old has finally brushed his teeth and found any socks that match. Emptying unfinished cereal bowls in the sink, she checks the clock one more time, knowing that if she changes the baby's diaper, the whole family will once again be late to church. The hardest part of the morning is containing her resentment against her husband, who has somehow found time to read the sports page while she has been expected to prepare herself and three crabby children. She'll have to put on lipstick in the car.

Across town a twenty-something young man presses his snooze alarm for the third time. Why did he cave in and agree to meet his friend at some church? To get the guy off his back after saying "No" on five other weekends. He wonders if it's too late to beg sickness, or if he should just get it over with and grab some coffee to give him a jolt and ease the slight hangover from last night's party.

A single dad honks the horn to pick up his fifth-grade son, hoping to give his boy a consistent religious experience and looking forward to their weekly donut stop after church. A grandmother carefully buttons her best dress and frets over the casual attire of most contemporary churchgoers. A thirty-two-year-old single woman catches herself smiling at a stoplight, filled with anticipation at the opportunity to go to church and thank God for the job promotion she thought would never come through.

A fifteen-year-old girl has fought with her mom all morning about why she had to get up so early on one of her only days off, why her skirt is too short to wear to church, and why a Diet Coke and half a donut aren't considered a nutritious breakfast. A young couple who have diligently prayed for a baby the last four years get into their sedan, longing to have need for a minivan someday. Going to church has become a painful reminder for them of the hole they feel, and they secretly hope they can emotionally handle the sight of so many happy families arriving in the parking lot.

Every Sunday morning a minority of people in your town and mine prepare to go to church. Each man, woman, and child has a story—a life that goes on from Monday through Saturday. Many of them rush to get to church on time. Some were on the fence all morning about whether they would really show up. So, for those who do arrive, who walk into a church and take a seat, what is at stake? How much does it really matter what takes place in the next hour?

Before we explore that question, we have to face reality. Getting people to church on Sundays is exceedingly difficult. That is true in the U.S., Australia, Europe, and most places around our world. In many cultures, church attendance is no longer considered normal, and most of the population never give it a thought. People have so many other attractive options on Sunday morning—sleeping in, lazily enjoying the paper, sports activities, errands, family outings, house projects. It is no longer much of a "should" in modern society to go to church. The majority don't go. Add to that the incredible pace of life and the assumption that a church service won't be worth the time.

That's sobering, hard-to-hear truth. *And yet*—there has rarely been a time when the local church has greater potential for spiritual impact! While people may not be coming to weekly services, we see a profound spiritual seeking in most places around the world. Many are facing the emptiness of a life without meaning. Countless families are in crisis, or wrestling with economic uncertainty. People are hungry for truth, for deep inner peace, for genuine community, for a sense of hope and raucous joy.

I have never believed more strongly in the potential of the hour on Sunday! From the moment the first note is played or the first word is spoken, opportunity hangs in the air. The hour can simply be sixty minutes for attenders to survive, a time for minds to wander aimlessly and hearts to go untouched. Or, just maybe, the hour on Sunday can be a time of wonder, a time of transformation, perhaps even a time of awe. That's precisely what the earliest Christians experienced. In Acts 2 we read that when those first believers gathered, "everyone was filled with awe." And beyond that, "the Lord added to their number *daily* those who were being saved" (empasis added). Now that's a picture of church that stirs my spirit.

Sadly, very few churchgoers—and certainly not those who are unchurched—would use words like *awe* to describe the hour in church on Sunday. Most would describe their experience at church as *tolerable* at best. Which adjectives does the world most often use to describe church? I have asked that question in Australia, Germany, Sweden, the United States, and several other countries. I always hear the same words: *Boring. Irrelevant. Mediocre. Hypocritical. Academic. Stuffy.* Few folks expect to be moved or encouraged or transformed in significant ways because of that hour on Sunday. We must face the reputation we are up against. Most people carry a very low opinion of church. Does this bother you as much as it bothers me? It makes me mad and pumps me up!

We have an enormous job to do. Certainly God must be grieved that his bride, the local church, is viewed with such apathy and disdain. Our God longs to use the gathering time in communities of faith for some of his greatest work in human hearts. We can't blame God for the mediocrity and lack of awe in our church services. He has not changed. He is always ready to pour out his supernatural, anointing power. But too often we have not done our part. We are called to carefully craft services that are packed with potential for God to do his mighty work. It is a cooperative effort—and many of us are not holding up our end of the deal. When we give God our absolute best and he sends his Spirit to touch lives, the possibilities are truly awesome!

It All Begins with Sundays

Weekend services at any local church drive every other part of the ministry. They are the big kahuna, the whole enchilada, the first impression, and the front door. Any biblically functioning community of faith has many important ministries. A healthy

Recipe: The whole Enchilada: Weekend Services
Ingredients: people
resources
leadership
vision
core values
Directions:
Layer the ingredients together, pray for 10 minutes at 98.6 degress and enjoy!

church cares for the poor and the sick, ministers to the youth and the elderly, helps people connect to one another in smaller groups, and reaches out to those far from God. But all these ministries depend on the weekend services to provide people, resources, leadership, vision, and core values. Our pastor sees the services as the funnel for all the rest of church work and often says, "As the weekend services go, so goes the church!" In almost every case, sub-ministries in the church lean on corporate gatherings to thrive.

Something very significant can happen when the body of Christ gathers all together on Sunday morning. Those weekly services define what matters to a church and its leaders, what they will focus on all week, what part of God's Word will challenge them, and how they'll experience God's supernatural presence and power. When Sunday mornings inspire, envision, and equip those who attend, a buzz of excitement is generated that feeds all the sub-ministries and events. If church leaders become complacent about carefully preparing the hour on Sunday, they jeopardize the church's entire life and mission.

How hot does my own zeal burn for God's house? How concerned am I when I see my own church fail to reach its full potential? Is my passion for the bride of Christ increasing or waning over time? These questions inspire me to periodically measure my zeal factor, and to care most about what God cares about—the establishment of his kingdom here on earth. I believe God is honored whenever we devote ourselves to improving our churches and to carefully planning weekend services that increasingly reflect his awesome power, grace, and love.

Recently, I have been challenged by the passion of Jesus himself for what takes place in God's house. In John 2, we read about Jesus' angry response toward those who had turned the temple courts into a strip mall, shamelessly marketing their livestock in a house of worship. To do justice to the scene described by John, we have to imagine Jesus on fire with disgust—this is not a portrait of a man nicely offering constructive criticism! Jesus crafted a whip, literally driving away offenders and boldly overturning their tables of commerce. His disciples must have been shocked. What a display of unbridled emotion, in front of casual shoppers, curious onlookers, and religious leaders who completely doubted his authority.

Jesus' actions reminded his disciples of a verse from the Psalms: "For zeal for your house consumes me, and the insults of those who insult you fall on me" (Psalm 69:9). Jesus could not stand by, watching his Father's house compromised in any way. He saw the temple as the gathering place for a community of faith, and it would not be long before the Son of God would describe the church as his "bride"—the ultimate treasure whose excellence and beauty must be upheld and cherished.

The hour on Sunday matters to me because it matters to God. During that hour, people are forming impressions of a faith community—but they are also forming impressions of God. We have an opportunity either to draw them closer to their heavenly Father or push them farther away. More than ever, I am convinced that modern day miracles can take place when people enter our churches. That sixty minutes can be a time of wonder, a time to quiet souls, spark deep emotion, and prompt turning points with eternal significance.

The Wonder of a Quieted Soul

The service's first potential wonder is the wonder of a quieted soul. How much time for quiet moments, outside of sleeping, does the average person have in our culture? Some of us who make time for solitude are simply out of touch with most people's daily lives.

All day long, folks are bombarded by noise and information. The technology explosion—including cell phones, PDAs (personal digital assistants), e-mail, and voice mail—has created a culture of people who are never out of reach. Add to that the relentless barrage of radio, television, magazines, the Internet, and stacks of books. The pace of our society keeps escalating. Everyone always seems to be in such a hurry!

So when people do come to church, they rarely arrive expecting to be still, to receive a touch of the divine. Most men and women have not experienced a quieting of their soul all week long. Even getting to church may feel frantic after navigating traffic and hunting for a decent parking place. In a sixty-minute service, we have the magnificent opportunity to give attenders an enormous gift—the gift of slowing down, encountering the presence of God, and wrestling with life's deeper issues. They can't reach such quiet immediately. Our job is to guide them there, and then pray that God will do his work.

I recently experienced my own soul being quieted at church. It happened at a Saturday evening service, after a day filled with a daughter's soccer game, errands, and house cleaning. I had not made any time for solitude or spiritual reflection. The theme of the service was community—that we were created from the beginning to long for significant connection with a few other people who truly know us and love us, even the nasty parts of ourselves we try to hide. Music early in the service began to prepare listeners by revealing songs in our culture that clearly express this desire for community. I felt my own pulse

g r a d u a l l y   s . . l . . . .o . . . . . w . . . . . . .i . . . . .n . . . .

down especially as I listened to a passionate recurring lyric: "I don't want to be an island anymore." And then the moment of stillness happened for me.

It came during a drama sketch of a man who lived much of his life in isolation, then risked tasting the power of connection in a small group. He joined the group because his new girlfriend insisted, and he laughed every time he heard the phrase "small group," because it was such a foreign term. Yet, that group of friends became extremely significant in his life. Through narrative we learned that the guy married the girlfriend, and they eventually moved out of state. Sadly, the marriage began to fall apart, and the man moved back to his hometown. One day he ran into one of that original circle of friends. I noticed, as the scene grew more serious, how quiet the audience became. Up on the platform, the small group invited this man to join them, and once again, made a circle to surround him with support. They accepted him just as he was.

The auditorium was still. No one coughed or moved a muscle. We were witnessing together a portrait of what we all long for. The Holy Spirit was at work, speaking to a diverse audience in many ways about our individual needs for authentic community. There was no applause when the drama ended. As our pastor came up to lead us in prayer and to teach, most of us had soft hearts ready to hear truth from God's Word. Though I'd rushed to hurry my family out the door, through traffic, and into the auditorium, my soul now felt much different—quiet and reflective.

Many people who attend church on Sunday morning haven't truly connected with God in a long time. Those of us privileged to prepare church services can offer attenders an opportunity—during the service—to be touched by God. Even for people just beginning their spiritual journey, this is an incredible gift. Author Garrison Keillor once said:

> If you can't go to church and, for at least a moment, be given transcendence. . . then I can't see why anyone should go. Just a brief moment of transcendence causes you to come out of church a changed person.

I contend that most people would consider the gift of a quieted soul well worth any time spent in church.

The Wonder of a Deeply Felt Emotion

The second amazing wonder possible on Sunday is the wonder of a deeply felt emotion. Most people do not expect to be moved by anything in church. Occasionally, they may feel deep emotions at a movie or a powerful theatrical production. But they most often assume that church will engage only their heads, not their hearts. So, if and when we help attenders access deep feelings, laugh from the gut, relate to something sad, or get angry about injustice—we serve them well. God designed all of us to be both thinkers *and* feelers. We definitely need to use our heads in church, to learn truths about God. But it is equally vital that we be moved. And the great news is that the arts have unbelievable potential to move human beings. I believe that is why God gave us the arts. Three images describe for me why the arts are wonderful: great art can be a signpost, a mirror, or a pair of shoes.

1

A Signpost

In his excellent book *Windows of the Soul*, Ken Gire writes, "God gave us art, music, sculpture, drama, and literature. He gave them as footpaths to lead us out of our hiding places and as signposts to lead us along in our search for what was lost." Art and beauty are some of God's most powerful tools to draw us toward a relationship with him. C.S. Lewis referred to great art as "drippings of grace" which can awaken in us a thirst for God. Just as the majesty of God's own creation pulls us toward knowing the Creator, art has the potential to move us deep in our souls.

Have you ever encountered a work of art that transfixed you and stirred spiritual longings? Throughout my life I have been blessed to witness powerful moments through the arts—in church and other arenas. I stood with a lump in my throat before the original Van Gogh painting *Starry Night*; I could not move after the painful conclusion of Brian Dennehy's Broadway performance of Willy Loman in *Death of a Salesman*; my spirit soared as I sat in the balcony and absorbed the Chicago Symphony Orchestra's music; I leapt to my feet to applaud the Hubbard Street Dance Company's joyful abandonment.

The sheer wonder and beauty of the arts provide moments when, as Elizabeth Barrett Browning wrote, "earth's crammed with heaven"!

Artists enable us to plumb the depths. Artists themselves hunger to know and understand the truth. Often they do not look at life with ordinary eyes—and so they offer us a window to deeper truth. Typically, artists are more honest than the rest of us about the pain of life and the agony of searching for God. Frederick Buechner wrote, "There would be a strong argument for saying that much of the most powerful preaching of our time is the preaching of the poets, playwrights, novelists, because it is often they better than the rest of us who speak with awful honesty about the absence of God in the world and about the storm of his absence. . . ."

Until we honestly acknowledge the pain of
this life, we cannot effectively unleash the arts
to point people toward the grace, beauty, and
truth of relationship with God. What
an incredible privilege to be a part of leveraging
the arts as a signpost!

A Mirror

"You use a glass mirror to see your face. You use works of art to see
your soul," said George Bernard Shaw. God can use works of art to
help you and me look deep inside, to see our longings more clearly,
and even to change the way we look at ourselves. Artists have a God-given
ability to view the human condition with lenses that cut to the heart. In
Thornton Wilder's play *Our Town*, the lead character, Emily, asks the Stage Manager,
"Do any human beings ever realize life while they live it—every, every minute?" The
Stage Manager replies, "No. The saints and poets, maybe—they do some." When we
experience a great work of art, it often opens a corner of our hearts we've ignored or
even smothered. That's what happened to me when I first saw the film *Schindler's List*.

I expected that movie to deeply move me about the horrors of the Holocaust, and
it did. What I did not expect was to get in touch with another longing of my soul. The
main character, Oscar Schindler, is based on a real man who set up a factory to protect
Jewish employees from being sent to concentration camps. Near the film's end, as Oscar
surveys his employees' grateful faces, he confides deep regrets to his co-leader. He wonders aloud about how many more lives he could have saved had he sold his car, jewelry,
or other possessions. The weight of comparing the value of human lives to temporary
riches overwhelms him—he condemns himself for not doing more.

Somehow the writer of that script tapped into my deep desire to make a difference
in this world, to not waste any resources, to avoid living with any regrets. The scene
profoundly inspired my husband and me. We talked afterwards of the stewardship principles Jesus taught in Matthew 25. The creators of the film, while they may not be

1

Christians, captured the essence of what it means to serve God and people with full devotion, to have an eternal perspective on what really matters. I will never forget the look in Oscar Schindler's eyes, wishing he had given more, knowing that nothing is worth more than a human life. What powerful preaching the arts can be! You and I can hold a mirror to our own souls, and then share that mirror to reflect the same longings in the souls of others.

A Pair of Shoes

Art can be a signpost, a mirror. . . or even a pair of shoes. What do I mean by that? Great art can give us a deeper understanding of another person's world, of the human situation. In his Nobel lecture on literature, Aleksander Solzhenitsyn said of art and literature:

Both hold the key to a miracle: to overcome man's ruinous habit of learning only from his own experience, so that the experience of others passes him by without profit. Making up for man's scant time on earth, art transmits between men the entire accumulated load of another being's life experiences with all its hardships, colors, and juices. It re-creates—life like—the experience of other men, so that we can assimilate it as our own.

Great art opens a window for us to understand the lives and struggles of others: *To Kill a Mockingbird. Roots. Anna Karenina. A Doll's House. Amadeus. Les Misérables. Children of a Lesser God. Forrest Gump. Night. Hoop Dreams.* The list goes on and on, and I haven't even touched on music, painting, or dance. But can art in a church service provide a pair of shoes, a point of identification?

Years ago, a close friend's experience inspired one of our drama writers to write a sketch that tied in with our pastor's message on unanswered prayer, part of a series on prayer. Our pastor wisely discerned that we need to be honest: some prayers do not get answered—at least not in the way we hope—and we wonder if God listens or cares. Our writer's drama sketch began with a young woman excitedly telling her friend about the expected arrival of a newborn infant she and her husband were going to adopt after years of infertility and disappointment. Then the husband showed up with horrible news. The birth mother had changed her mind. There would be no baby. As the wife tried to absorb this news, she grew increasingly upset, throwing her friend's gift, a new baby outfit, on the couch. She launched into a tirade, shouting these honest words when her husband told her to calm down: "I don't want to calm down! I'm angry. I hate that girl. I hate you. I hate me.

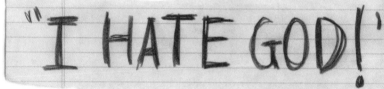

I hate everybody. I hate this,
I hate this, I hate this!" She broke down sobbing in her husband's arms.

Is it okay to hear anyone, even an actress, say in church that they hate God? That sketch really resonated with people. It didn't end in a pretty package. It was so real. How many of us have had such thoughts when life does not go according to plan, when God seems distant and uncaring, and we are bombarded with loss and disappointment? That sketch helped us face together that much of life remains a mystery. The arts gave us a pair of shoes, and together we experienced the painful emotions of loss and wrestling with God. The drama prepared us to open ourselves to the message time, to hear truth about a God who does care and will be with us even in life's most severe storms.

The wonder of deeply felt emotions in church sometimes leads to a more amazing wonder. Lives sometimes change for eternity in that hour on Sunday.

The Wonder of a Turning Point

At the end of the day, our church services are all about life change. If people drive away on Sunday mornings no different from when they came in, we haven't accomplished anything that matters. We're aiming for an enormous goal. We want people to *make decisions*. These decisions vary widely. For some, it might be a next step in character growth, or a new resolve about exhibiting more love as a parent, spouse, or friend. Someone else might choose to pray to God for the first time in a long time. Maybe another person attempts to worship and commits to the awkward early stages of expressing praise to God. The turning point might be confession. A few individuals might make a decision to cross the line of faith. True decision results in action, in real life change from Monday through Saturday. Whenever I see or hear about actual growth *in real people*, I rededicate myself again to the wonder of Sundays.

My husband and I became friends with Fred and Linda while our daughters played on a traveling soccer team. Travel sports involve hours on the sidelines and out-of-town tournaments with people who become a surrogate family. We'd had several months of connection before I discovered that Fred and Linda had been casually checking out our church. Fred had drifted from the church of his youth after a divorce. Our team was preparing an outreach event to offer a point of entry for people just like Fred and Linda. I invited them to drive with my husband and me to the event.

As we returned to the parking lot, I observed tears in Fred's eyes. I wasn't sure if he had allergies or had been deeply moved by the music, drama, and dance. It turned out he was moved! Fred told us later that he went home that night and talked to God for the first time in years. He had recently lost his corporate sales position and was struggling to find peace. Over several months, we had many spiritual conversations that ultimately led to

oh, how i love baptism services!

Congratulations:
May God bless you on this very special day. We love you!
Nancy + Warren

both Fred and Linda committing their lives to Jesus Christ. They asked my husband and me to participate in their baptism on a warm June afternoon in the lake at Willow Creek. At that moment, I thought my heart would burst. A combination of personal relationship, the hours on Sunday, and the undeniable power of the Holy Spirit all led to this precious couple making a decision that will matter forever!

from left to right:
warren, linda's sister, me,
linda, and fred

Willow Creek Community Church
BAPTISMS

Our God is in the business of changing human hearts. For reasons we may never fully comprehend until heaven, he has chosen to partner with the likes of us. In 2 Corinthians 5:19 we read that God "has committed to us the message of reconciliation." The hour on Sunday can be a vital part of bringing people into a genuine relationship with their Creator. We are called to prepare services that have the greatest potential for human beings to quiet their souls, to feel emotions deeply, and to choose growth and change. What a privilege and awesome responsibility we hold!

"I Was Born for This"

I stand in awe of a God who not only rescued us from sin, but who also guides us to discover our spiritual gifts and fills us with passion for a lifelong journey of service. My own journey began as a little girl in a neighborhood filled with children. I delighted in producing elaborate productions, including a backyard circus, a gruesome haunted house, and several plays and musicals. "Let's put together a show!" was my favorite expression, and I most often served as the driving force behind our creative efforts. Those early explorations of the arts and what I now recognize as a leadership gift were followed by a focus on theater and contest speaking in high school.

And then a major turning point came when I was about fifteen years old. Our student ministry at church, a very typical group of about thirty students, began to study God's Word with greater intensity under the guidance of a new youth pastor. We became captivated by a genuine and growing love for Jesus, along with a disturbing awareness that far too many of our school friends were unaware of God's love for them. Our leaders—Bill Hybels and Dave Holmbo—suggested we create a weekly experience for our friends, one that could communicate the truths of Christianity in a way they could understand and be compelled to consider.

So what could I bring to that party? I tentatively offered to assemble a small group of friends to create drama presentations for those weekly events. I had absolutely no idea what that would involve or how to begin. Our early efforts were clumsy and mediocre. But every so often I saw music, drama, and visual presentations powerfully prepare students to hear Bill's relevant, biblical message. And whenever it worked—when I saw God move—I could hardly sleep when my head hit the pillow! One night my biology lab partner gave her life to Christ, along with many others. From those days on, I knew God made me to somehow combine the arts and biblical teaching to create experiences through which the Spirit could touch lives. What an amazing gift, to discover at the age of fifteen why God put me on this planet—to know the unspeakable joy of being used to make a difference.

Thirty years later, I still can't get over the wonder of what God has enabled me to do. I have the profound privilege of building a community of artists who together unleash the arts in our church. Our goal has always been to prepare for the possibility for God to anoint our work, resulting in what we call *transcendent moments*. My journey has not been without struggle or disappointment. Many days I have considered giving up. But there have been even more weeks when I witness what those early believers experienced—times when we are "filled with awe." I have dedicated my life to creating hours on Sunday that are filled with potential to transform human lives, as we partner with the Almighty God.

More than anything, this book is a collection of what I have learned so far, lessons gained through mistakes and defeats. Any team that seeks to create effective church

services builds their ministry on core values. This book describes the values I believe are most significant in an arts ministry. The first half, "Getting Ready for Sundays," explores behind-the-scenes, foundation-building values. The second half, "Riding Home from Sundays," focuses on values that help attenders experience services filled with meaning and power.

As I write, I am most concerned with what is timeless and should always be true, no matter what kind of church applies these values, no matter what generation we seek to reach. To be honest, my "target audience" has in many ways been my two young daughters. I imagine them twenty years from now, possibly serving in an arts ministry in a local church somewhere. (They both exhibit early signs of loving the arts.) No doubt they will face a culture far different from the one I sought to reach, and even from the one I see today. As our society becomes increasingly postmodern and our basic worldview changes, church ministries must adjust strategies. Therefore, this book is not about the nitty-gritty details of how to put together your church service. It is all about what matters most as you go about that glorious task. My prayer for you, the reader, is that our God will captivate, inspire, encourage, and challenge you to dedicate yourself even more fully to the adventure of creating the hour on Sunday.

Questions to Explore

1. On a scale of 1 to 10, how would you rate your own personal zeal for the potential power of the "Hour on Sunday?" What will be required for your passion to increase?

2. Recall a time when your own soul was quieted through an experience at church. What happened that enabled you to slow down and connect with God?

3. List a few of your own encounters with music, theater, or any other art form that deeply moved you. Can you name your top three?

4. Evaluate the frequency with which you see geniune life change in attenders as a result of coming to your weekly church services. How are people different when they leave from when they walked in?

chapter two

As a
planner
of church
services
and events,
I certainly
do not
want to
be part
of any
hour on
Sunday that
fails to
reach its
potential or
connect with
its audience.

Intentionality

WHAT ARE WE TRYING TO DO AND WHO ARE WE TRYING TO REACH?

My thirteen~year~old daughter, Samantha, still raves about the birthday party we gave when she turned five. Although I take no credit for the creativity of that event—I stole all the ideas from *Family Fun* magazine—I did my best to execute it well. The party had a castle theme, complete with princesses, an evil dragon, and food appropriate for royalty. As any parent knows, designing a two-hour party for five-year-olds requires more planning and careful execution than any big-time event for adults. Otherwise, those two hours can seem like a chaotic eternity! Children look forward to their parties with enormous expectations, and I certainly did not want to fail.

As a thirty-something mom, I had to imagine the entire experience through a five-year-old girl's eyes. What would Samantha's young guests like to eat—or avoid like the plague? What games would fully entertain them for at least ten minutes? How should the little ones be asked to dress? What take-home trinkets might excite them? One of my proudest moments as a domestically challenged mom was creating a castle cake that looked exactly like the one in the magazine, complete with candy turrets and a licorice drawbridge that spanned the moat of icing. Only those who know me well can fully appreciate how that endeavor terrified me! My husband, Warren, was just as proud of the castle he crafted out of a huge furniture box. It provided a safe haven for children screaming with delight while he pretended to be the evil dragon. The best part of the day was seeing the shining eyes of our little princess who had so much fun and was visibly proud of what she thought was the best birthday party ever.

Any event that hits the mark for its audience does not just happen. Planners must be fully aware of exactly what they hope to accomplish and who their audience is. These principles are as true for the hour on Sunday as they are for birthday parties.

A well-planned service can make people respond the way my daughter did to her birthday party. Unfortunately, too many of us have attended church services that left us wondering if *anyone* had carefully planned it. At worst, the service feels haphazard, has no coherent theme, and belies a misguided attempt to reach just about everyone. All too often, no one is truly touched, transformed, or convinced the sixty minutes was worth their time.

An Awesome Celebration

As a planner of church services and events, I certainly do not want to be part of any hour on Sunday that fails to reach its potential or connect with its audience. Nehemiah 12 inspires me. The prophet planned a worship celebration following Israel's return from exile. He led the children of Israel to rebuild the wall of Jerusalem—a huge undertaking—in just fifty-two days. After the physical work was done, the people gathered to confess and recommit themselves to obeying God. Nehemiah relates that Levites (special priests) and singers were "sought out from where they lived and were brought to Jerusalem to celebrate joyfully the dedication with songs of thanksgiving and with the music of cymbals, harps and lyres."

The text describes an astoundingly complex service that included two enormous choirs to lead the people in giving thanks. Both choirs progressed along the top of the wall—one from the right, the other from the left. The two choirs met in the middle and proceeded inside the house of God. Jezrahiah, the man who led the choirs, orchestrated this massive event without microphones, headset communication, or printed rehearsal plans. (Imagine producing the opening ceremonies of the Olympics without such technology.) Yet somehow the entire experience worked so effectively that "the sound of rejoicing in Jerusalem could be heard far away." What a glorious spectacle of praise that must have been! I am convinced the children of Israel never forgot the wonder of that day. The planners' hard work and participants' passion came together in a service that deeply moved those who attended. I believe that Nehemiah and the other planners clearly understood the service's purpose and audience. Thousands of years later, we have much to emulate and learn from this Old Testament prophet.

Although most of us prefer to direct our energies to the creative, fun part of planning the hour on Sunday, this chapter explores the hard, but absolutely essential, work of clearly defining three things: our church's mission, our strategy for weekly services, and our primary audience.

Defining Your Church's Mission

Every effective ministry team—including the arts team—can express in a sentence exactly what their local church is called to do. Having a clear mission statement provides a tremendous sense of unity and freedom because everyone understands what they are trying to accomplish and who they are trying to reach. At Willow Creek, we've worked hard to make sure every person at our church's core knows precisely what we are about: "turning irreligious people into fully devoted followers of Christ." We also have a clearly articulated strategy for accomplishing this mission in our community. Our mission and strategy capture our ministry thumbprint, the unique characteristics of God's call for our church. Our pastor often says that each local church must discern its own ministry thumbprint.

Although not every church is called to the same mission or strategy, every church is called to prayerfully consider what kind of community God is calling them to be. There isn't just one right answer! As the Apostle Paul made clear in 1 Corinthians 12, "There are different kinds of service in the church, but it is the same Lord we are serving. There are different ways God works in our lives, but it is the same God who does the work through all of us" (1 Corinthians 12:5–6 NLT). Knowing their precise mission gives staff and the volunteer arts team a wonderful sense of freedom and focus. They'll still need animated dialog to interpret *how* to live out that mission, but the church's core leaders will know deep inside what God has asked them to do and what they can leave for other ministries. *No effective church can be all things to all people.*

A church's mission most often reflects the unique gifts and strengths of its key leaders, especially the senior pastor. The gift of evangelism is the primary strength and passion of our founding leader, Bill Hybels. As a result, our church has always emphasized reaching lost people and finding ways to bring them into an environment where they can investigate Christianity. Robert Guerrero, senior pastor of Iglesia Comunitaria Cristiana in the Dominican Republic, has a passion to provide holistic ministry to the poor who live near the church in Santo Domingo. Iglesia Comunitaria Cristiana is strategically designed to bring people to faith by first meeting basic needs for food, job training, and childcare. The church even provides a gym where local folks can exercise for a nominal fee and also meet believers.

The responsibility for crafting and defining a church's mission typically rests with the pastor, elders, or other governing bodies. Many leadership teams use group retreats to prayerfully define God's thumbprint for their ministry. The ideal mission statement should inspire people with a

CLEAR VISION

of why the church exists. It should be brief enough to be easily learned, remembered, and repeated. For example, "to help people become so excited about Christ that they share him with every person in their sphere of influence" is the mission statement of Woodmen Valley Chapel in Colorado Springs, Colorado.

Strategy for Weekly Services

After establishing a clear mission, the next step is developing strategies to accomplish that mission. Any healthy church will no doubt include several kinds of ministries to become a fully functioning biblical community. This book focuses on strategies tied specifically to the purpose of weekly gatherings and how they connect to the church's overall mission. The best way I know to illustrate this important process is to take a page from the history of our church.

Nearly thirty years ago, our church's humble beginnings as a student ministry included several strategic planning discussions. That was God's grace, because we didn't really recognize that's what we were doing!

When a group of young people founded Willow Creek, we were compelled to reach nonchurched people in our suburban community. For three years our youth ministry offered two experiences each week—one for our lost friends from school and another for our own worship and growth. So when it came time to start the church, we chose to replicate that model. On weekends, we created what we called a seeker service. We believed that if our nonchurched friends would ever come to a church service, they would most likely show up on a Sunday morning. The seeker service was designed to do two things: communicate the basic truths of Christianity in relevant ways our nonchurched friends could understand; and provide believers with a meaningful experience. This decision was a clear departure from what most of us grew up with. Sunday had always been a time for believers to gather and worship, and we were taking an enormous risk by changing it.

Would Christians willingly give up their extended worship hour on Sunday for an experience designed to reach friends far from God? We believed they would—if we provided a worship service at another time and cast the vision so believers could understand our strategy. (This approach did not appeal to all believers, and some elected to attend churches with a more conventional strategy.) We created a mid-week service for believers called *The New Community*. In this service we unashamedly target Christians with a ninety-minute combination of corporate worship and extensive teaching from God's Word. We also celebrate the sacrament of communion once a month and communicate issues strategic to our church's core of believers. Although it took—and takes—a lot of work to execute two kinds of services each week, their clearly defined focuses make planning them easier than trying to reach many goals in just one hour on Sunday.

In recent years it has become common for churches to define themselves—and other churches—by their strategy for weekly services. For example, people will often describe their church with phrases such as

seeker-targeted, seeker sensitive, or believer-targeted. *phrases*

As shorthand within church circles, such phrases provide a starting point for understanding a church's overall mission and strategy. However, it is important to avoid the danger of oversimplifying concepts and strategies that are actually quite complex. With this understanding, I want to explore the three most common kinds of churches and the strategies behind their services. As you read each description, consider which one most closely resembles your church's strategy for weekly services. Remember: though there is no right or wrong answer, your church needs to be very clear about its aims.

Seeker-Targeted Services

The primary focus of the seeker-targeted service is to offer a weekly experience for spiritual seekers who are not in a relationship with God. Willow Creek's weekend services fall into this broad category. We design weekend services—music decisions, artistic choices, language, sermon topics, and even our announcements—by imagining them through the eyes of someone far from God. This can be every bit as challenging as trying to figure out what five-year-old girls would enjoy at a birthday party!

And here's the trickiest part. While targeting nonbelievers, we also aim to thrill believers. That sounds like a huge contradiction, but we believe it is essential to our mission. Since most believers do not bring a nonchurched friend with them every week, it is vital that the service also minister to these Christians, feeding their souls and inspiring them to return Sunday after Sunday. Otherwise believers wouldn't show up unless they had a seeker at their side. Our weekly challenge is to design a service tailored for a person who has not been to church in years, while at the same time ministering effectively to long-term Christians. (No wonder so many members of our programming team are prematurely gray.)

Seeker-Sensitive Services

Seeker-sensitive churches essentially design a weekend worship and learning experience for Christians, but do so aware that seekers may be present. Because few of these churches have an alternate mid-week service designed exclusively for believers, they prepare what is often described as a "blended service." My friend Caron Loveless at Discovery Church in Orlando, Florida, leads the charge to design these kinds of experiences for their growing congregation. Their Sunday services include meaningful worship and creative use of the arts to communicate to believers and their seeking friends. They do not have a separate and distinct mid-week service.

Guiding veteran Christians to a time of authentic worship while still being sensitive to those who do not yet know God is a daunting task.

These leaders are always discerning how to serve those in the family of God, while not alienating those outside the family. They hope visitors will glimpse Christians engaging in authentic worship and thus be drawn toward God. Caron says that one key to their ministry's effectiveness is that the senior pastor (her husband, David) speaks to both audiences: "He's been a student of our culture, and he uses illustrations that anyone can relate to."

Believer-Targeted Services

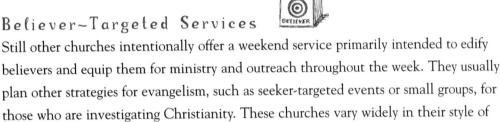

Still other churches intentionally offer a weekend service primarily intended to edify believers and equip them for ministry and outreach throughout the week. They usually plan other strategies for evangelism, such as seeker-targeted events or small groups, for those who are investigating Christianity. These churches vary widely in their style of worship—from a high-church, liturgical approach to a more informal service incorporating a wide spectrum of musical styles.

Recently, I treasured the experience of visiting Bethel Lutheran Church, a predominantly African-American congregation that gathers in a beautiful, stained-glass sanctuary over 100 years old on Chicago's west side. Their hour on Sunday—actually, more like two or three hours!—is a delightful mix of traditional Lutheran liturgy and their own touches. We heard the spoken Word through three Scripture lessons, read together the Nicene Creed, and were given the opportunity to partake in the sacrament of communion. But we also heard a passionate choir sing their hearts out on a song that soared with the recurring phrase, "My soul loves Jesus!" That moment touched me deeply, as I saw the vocalists' genuine love for Christ and reflected on my own devotion to Jesus. During the "passing of the peace," almost everyone there hugged and welcomed me. They call themselves the "friendliest church in the world," and I think they may be right. As their wonderful pastor, Maxine Washington, exclaimed, "It's a good day in church!"

There is certainly some overlap within these categories, and some churches may discern an altogether different paradigm for their service. Note that defining the kind of services you are called to create is not based on the type of art forms you use; for example, using drama or contemporary music does not necessarily mean you are a seeker-targeted church. Most essential is discerning your primary audience.

The overarching themes of these three approaches are:

- *Seeker-targeted services.* Designed to reach nonchurched people, while thrilling and inspiring believers. These churches usually offer a separate and distinct worship service for believers at another time during the week.
- *Seeker-sensitive services.* Primary objective is to engage and edify believers without alienating seekers, creating moments for the seeker to enter in. Usually do not have another weekly worship service.
- *Believer-targeted services.* Offer an experience for believers, while strategizing for evangelism through other ministries or events.

	CATEGORY	PRIMARY TARGET AUDIENCE	GOAL
SEEKER	Seeker-Targeted	Seekers	To enable seekers to learn the basic truths of Christianity and accept Christ while also thrilling believers
SEEKER BELIEVER	Seeker-Sensitive	Believers *(knowing that seekers might be present)*	To edify believers without alienating seekers
BELIEVER	Believer-Targeted	Believers	To equip and encourage believers

Once again, *there is no one right way to do ministry.* What matters is that everyone on the leadership team—including pastors, elders, church staff, and key volunteers—is absolutely clear about what your church aims to accomplish with its public services and events.

Defining Your Audience

Knowing whether we aim primarily to reach believers, seekers, or both enables a church to move from defining a mission to defining the audience for each kind of service. But it is only the beginning. We have found it extremely helpful to further discern our strategy by becoming students of our target audience. The phrase "target audience" makes people understandably nervous, because it sounds too much like Madison Avenue and implies that some people may be unwelcome. And if either connotation characterized what I mean by target audience, I would be very nervous, too. Clearly, God and the church are never to be treated like commodities to be hawked with Madison Avenue tactics. Nor should anyone seeking God ever be made to feel unwelcome in a church. As the body of Christ, the church is called to the highest standards of honoring God and honoring those who walk through our doors. We are called to create inclusive communities characterized primarily by our radical love for one another.

Defining a target audience is not about using tactics that dishonor God or alienate others. Defining a target audience simply means more completely understanding who God calls us to reach within our local community. Absolutely anyone who walks in the doors of a local church should be welcome to attend that service. One Willow Creek motto is that "all people matter to God." But if we attempt to plan and design services that will effectively reach *everyone*, we will most likely fail. Wise leaders become students of the culture in which their church is planted. They prayerfully discern who their ministry can most effectively target. Thus, target audience is not about deciding who gets to come. It's about having a framework for understanding the best way to reach people in your immediate community.

Acts 17 offers a tremendous example of understanding and aiming to reach a specific audience. The Apostle Paul was invited to address Epicurean and Stoic philosophers during one of their animated meetings at the Areopagus. Very familiar with this particular community, Paul was "greatly distressed to see that the city was full of idols" (Acts 17:16). He therefore began his message by connecting to his listeners' spiritual sensitivity. "People of Athens!" he called out, "I see that in every way you are very religious." Referring to their altar "To An Unknown God," Paul masterfully revealed to them the truth about a God who can be known. He carefully chose his words and reasoning, fully aware that his highly intelligent audience loved wrestling with philosophical ideas. At the end of the day, many in Paul's audience asked to hear him again, and a few actually came to faith. If this audience had been primarily fishermen, or Jewish religious leaders, or little children, Paul undoubtedly would have used an entirely different approach. He knew his target audience and uniquely tailored his approach to their needs.

Defining your target audience includes clearly understanding their **age range, spiritual temperature, and cultural traits**. Because communities are dynamic and always changing, leadership teams must periodically review their assumptions and make adjustments. For example, what was once an area full of young families may over time transition to a more mature community. To continue effectively meeting community needs, a church would likely need to adjust its strategy. The spiritual appetite of a generation or culture often shifts, as do other key traits that will profoundly affect how we do ministry.

Age Range

Our church was begun by young Baby Boomers convinced that our parents' methods could not reach our friends effectively. A couple decades later, I began to hear whisperings that some twenty-somethings at Willow Creek felt they were not being effectively ministered to by our methods. At first, I was in denial, thinking that it must be a few unhappy campers, certainly not a trend to be concerned about. But then the quiet whisperings turned into an actual meeting where I was confronted with reality.

A few representatives of what was then called Generation X had the audacity to tell our leadership team that our music was not optimal for reaching them and their friends, that our overall style of communication needed adjustments for their age group, and that they would prefer more message illustrations that captured their generation's challenges. **As I desperately tried to appear calm and under complete control, my defensiveness raged inside.** I had to take a deep breath and bite my tongue before saying something I might regret. I thought we had cracked a code that was timeless, that we would always be considered contemporary and cutting-edge. How dare these young upstarts imply that we could possibly be aging and out of touch! But I was wrong. Young people most often search for a ministry style that feels tailored for them, including music choices, message illustrations, and overall approach. This has been true for centuries (it prompted our own ministry's launch) and will likely prove to be the case for years to come.

Therefore, I urge planning teams to be aware of the age range they hope to reach. This can certainly include a span of fifteen to twenty-five years, but the truth is that none of us will effectively minister to both eighty-somethings *and* teens. By God's grace, we hope to draw from people on either side of our target age range. But defining the heart of the age range we aim for will help us decide how to design services. As television and Hollywood film producers have shown, though some series or films succeed at reaching a mass audience, most long-running shows or effective theatrical releases are written and produced for a niche audience. Granted, a church service is much different than a movie or television show, but the principle of discerning an audience profile is worth emulating. Too many ministry leaders refuse to concede that it is necessary to "do business" like those in the secular world. They believe they can simply count on the Spirit to enable our churches to reach everyone. While I affirm that absolutely nothing is impossible with God, I do think our Creator intends for us to lead our churches with all the wisdom and intelligence we can offer—and sometimes that means taking lessons from those in the world.

We must continually define the age group God has called us to reach. Some churches may choose to keep growing with the

not under complete control

under complete control

generation they started aiming for, while others will sense the Spirit leading them to retool their ministry for a younger group. In an ideal world, most of us would love to think we can all be together, the young and the old, worshiping side by side with unity and joy. I do believe that occasionally worshiping together shows us the awesome breadth of the body of Christ.

We humans strongly desire worship settings with song leaders and teaching attuned to our generation's language and unique style. Most of us appreciate the church's rich history of music and stories about heroes of faith; yet, entering a time warp is not the best way for attenders to receive truth during the hour on Sunday. Jesus himself was always relevant to his culture and audience, illustrating with everyday images his listeners could readily relate to. Wherever we find ourselves set in history and culture, we must do no less—always discerning forms and methods most likely to connect with our audience and personally engage them with God.

Spiritual Temperature

Every man, woman, and child is somewhere along a continuum of spiritual temperature. They range from atheists, who totally deny the existence of God, to fully devoted followers (or at least those who passionately aim to be!).

Atheist   Fully devoted

follower

As we define the audience God calls us to reach, we must wrestle with where they fall on the spiritual continuum. Early on at Willow Creek, our pastor made clear we were not targeting those he called the "acidly nonchurched." Such individuals need to be dragged to church and often carry huge chips on their shoulders against God and anything close to Christianity. By God's grace, a few such folks have come to faith through our ministry, but we are not intentionally targeting them. We discerned that our ministry would aim for those who are a little farther to the right on the continuum, at least beginning to explore spiritual things. They wonder if God exists, and, if so, how he feels about them. Our church's strategy relies heavily on relationships—believers building significant friendships with their nonchurched friends, leading, we hope, to spiritual conversations. As a result, most of our visitors come with a friend they trust, someone they believe truly cares for them. This makes all the difference in the world! Regardless of their spiritual baggage, they show up with someone they respect, someone who has invested in their life. This relational bond creates an initial openness to the things of God.

We also know that, increasingly, most of our target audience has very little biblical knowledge or training in basic Christian truths. They do not know the stories of Joseph, the transformation in a man named Saul, or even the Lord's Prayer. While we are careful to make very few assumptions about their understanding of the faith, neither do we want to insult their intelligence. In contrast, our mid-week believer service jumps right into biblical study and aims for those farther along. For each service type or event, your church must gauge the target audience's place along the spiritual temperature continuum. The team entrusted to plan that service will be forever grateful for clarity as they make content decisions.

Cultural Traits

It is vital for us to study the culture we seek to reach. Once again, Jesus is our example. He tailored his message to the unique experiences and circumstances of those to whom he spoke—farmers, tax gatherers, spiritual leaders, or fishermen. We will have greater effectiveness if we can describe with increasing accuracy the kinds of folks we aim to reach. Effectively reaching our audience requires asking:

- What education level do most of the people have?
- What are the most common industries or types of occupations?

- What is the average income?
- What is the racial demographic mix?
- What needs and issues are most prevalent?
- What kinds of music does this group listen to? What are their favorite radio stations? What television shows, newspapers, and magazines top their list?
- What percentage is single? What percentage is married?
- Which hobbies or pastimes are popular?

Wrestling with such questions helps a ministry planning team enormously. We understand those sitting in our church on Sunday morning, as well as those we long to reach but who choose not to come.

Consequently, a rural church in Sibley, Iowa, may create a service with a far different approach and feel than a Boston inner-city church or a community in the Phoenix suburbs.

Once a creative team has a firm grasp on who they aim to reach, the adventure of creative service planning begins. For example, our weekend service targets both married and single adults in the thirty to fifty-five age range. Through surveys and other means, we have discovered a nearly equal split between single and married. This requires us to avoid exclusively addressing one audience or another through our drama sketches, video pieces, and message illustrations. Because most of our planning team and teaching pastors are married, we must often remind one another of all the single adults among us, and plan accordingly. We've sometimes leaned too far toward married attenders and were not as inclusive as we should have been of those divorced, widowed, or never married. The better our grasp on current and potential audiences, the more we will prayerfully and intentionally create services that help attenders conclude, "I felt like they were talking straight to me!"

One of Willow Creek's most recent challenges concerns the growing racial diversity of our community. When we began, Willow Creek's surrounding population was almost entirely Caucasian. Demographics have changed dramatically within a twenty-minute drive of our church. We now aim to become a more diverse community, and we're learning what will be required for us to effectively reach people from a wider variety of backgrounds. Our leadership team, up-front communicators, and all our ministries will change as we diversify.

As I visit churches, I see vivid disparity among ministry teams. Those who understand what they are trying to do and who they are trying to reach exhibit unity and freedom in designing weekly services. Teams that are fuzzy on their **purpose** are often frustrated and confused. Mastering this foundational value prepares teams to address the next chapter's question: What kind of services should we create?

1. What is your church's mission statement? What is your church aiming to do, and who is it trying to reach?

2. How many public services do you have each week? Can you clearly define what each service is intended to accomplish? If not, what steps need to be taken?

3. Write a paragraph that describes the age range, spiritual temperature, and cultural traits of your main target audience. What do you know about these individuals? How similar are they to you? Are you planning for a group of people vastly different from yourself?

Jack,
This chapter is getting too long. What should I do?
Nancy

Nancy,
Just create another chapter... no one will ever know. Ha-ha!
Jack

chapter **three**

As long
as I live,
I will
never get
over what
a glorious,
holy
adventure
we engage
in as we
plan the
hour on
Sunday and
partner with
our heavenly
Father!

Intentionality

WHAT KIND OF SERVICES SHOULD WE CREATE?

I confess that when I drive to my own church on Sunday morning, my mind is usually absorbed with rehearsal—or, more specifically and selfishly, *my part in the service*. But occasionally, God leads me to take the focus off myself. My mind wanders to other churches gathering on that day, to friends serving communities around the world. I wonder about plans for services in the Woodlands of Texas; Canandaigua, New York; and southern England. I sometimes offer a prayer for others involved with services, just as I am. Thousands upon thousands of local churches all around the world will assemble for an hour or more. If we could magically drop in to sample the tremendous variety in approach, style, and subject matter, the diversity would blow us away. Our options are unlimited!

Thumb through any magazine on church life and you will be struck by vast opportunities to attend workshops and read books about doing church more effectively. So, how do we design services best for our individual church? Given our mission and target audience, what should we plan for the hour on Sunday? The second essential phase of intentionality requires us to focus on three parts of service planning: series selection, style selection, and casting.

Intentional Series Selection

Many churches organize their service calendar around themes or series—such as a topical focus or section of scripture. Whether we like it or not, both believers and seekers often decide to attend church based on how much the title of the service or series appeals to them. Does the title capture their attention? Is it something they care about? Will it be worth their time? Knowing this, it is exceedingly important to be very intentional when choosing message topics and titles.

Recently I was invited to a private home to talk with perceptive volunteers and staff members about our church's upcoming season of weekend services. We sat on comfortable couches or cross-legged on the soft carpet, sipping lemonade and nibbling from small plates of snacks. Our task was to brainstorm for two hours about possible message topics, series, and titles. Our weekend director led the session and our pastor took careful notes and contributed ideas. I loved the energy in the room as we discussed current issues in our culture, what truths our nonchurched friends most need to hear, and what topics would appeal most to both believers and seekers. Our pastor has always taken tremendous care with this process. To make these crucial choices, he goes on his knees before God and seeks input from elders, staff, and key volunteers. Like many churches, we build our services around the teaching subjects, whether a topical series or a study of a particular book of the Bible. Series length varies from two weeks to an entire ministry season, depending on the goal of the services and the target audience.

Certain subjects and series rarely fail to draw a crowd. When John and Nancy Ortberg were both on our staff, John liked to tease his wife, who led Axis (our Next-Gen ministry), that they consistently focused on only three subjects: **sex, the end times, and will there be sex in the end times?** Whether we like it or not, many attenders decide whether to come based on how well the subject matter meets a felt need. This could include a series on marriage, finding a mate, finances, dealing with anger, parenting, or the problem of pain.

The Bible teaches us that we should "not give up meeting together, as some are in the habit of doing" (Hebrews 10:25 NIV). We call this the discipline of assembly, and we teach believers that they should build into their life rhythms the regular practice of attending services whenever our congregation gathers together—it's important to just show up! As Christians mature, attending weekly services should become a deeply ingrained practice no matter what subject the service covers. But newer believers and nonchurched people haven't yet developed this discipline. We must face this reality and recognize that message and series titles matter. It does no good to wish it were not so—we must do the hard work of crafting the series and titles that can attract an indecisive audience who may be sitting on the fence Sunday morning, deciding whether or not to get in the car.

Of course, we don't limit series selection to popular, crowd-pleasing subjects that meet felt needs. There is much biblical truth that people need to hear but that will never be high on anyone's list of favorite topics or safe subjects. For example, a few years back we discerned that we needed to address head-on the issue of sin and how it destroys each one of us. But we knew that inviting someone to a series titled *Sin* probably wouldn't fill our parking lot. So our pastor creatively titled the series

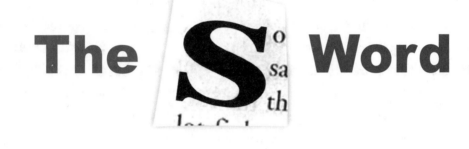

People were intrigued enough to wonder just which "S word" he had in mind. They showed up in good numbers. Some may call this a bait-and-switch approach, but sometimes a good title can help a church to explore difficult truths that simply must be addressed. Some of my favorite titles have included: *Strength for the Storms of Life*, *Graduate-Level Loving*, *Seasons of the Soul*, and *Getting this Christmas Right*.

We have also learned to be intentional about the balance between what we call *vertical series* and *horizontal series*. A vertical message series focuses primarily on some aspect of our relationship to God—his identity, the basics of salvation, character traits God desires in us. Horizontal series emphasize human relationships, including parenting, friendship, marriage, and dealing with anger. Ministry teams must discern an appropriate balance of vertical and horizontal series when planning their yearly calendar. One fall we planned a long vertical series about the identity of God. Each week we explored one aspect of God's nature, and it definitely stretched and grew our congregation. When that series was completed, people were hungry for something different, something a little more connected to their everyday lives. In response, that spring we launched into a horizontal series about family issues and relationships.

Seasons have a huge impact on whether a series works well. During September in Chicago, everyone focuses on getting back to school, work, and regular routines after summer. The entire community anticipates re-engaging and getting their act together. In many ways, September seems more like the start of the year than January does. One year we mistakenly scheduled a series titled *Modern Day Madness* in September. The goal was to explore difficult issues—pornography, homosexuality, and abortion, to name a few. While the series content was strong, it proved to be much too dark for September, when most attenders prefer to focus on new beginnings. If we could redo it, we might schedule that series for late fall or winter. We blew it big time.

January in Chicago means two things: New Year's resolutions and terrible weather. We have found it to be an excellent month to dig into message series that address ordering our lives in the areas of finances, physical fitness, time management, and spiritual disciplines. If we tried that series in the blistering hot month of July, when everyone is interested in relaxing with family and friends, we would have a mutiny on our hands! Church leaders experiment and learn these kinds of rhythms over time. It is helpful to look back over a ministry year and evaluate together which series were placed just right and which ones might have worked better at another time.

I urge you to not allow any one person to make the crucial decisions of topics and series for your services. Pastors and programming directors should seek input from creative, perceptive folks who have a pulse on your community and who understand and embrace your mission. You might consider taking a select group to a one-day retreat for the sole purpose of looking at your ministry year, brainstorming, and praying over these critical decisions.

Did you know the didgeridoo is believed to be the world's oldest wind instrument? Its origins can be traced back thousands of years to North Australian aborigines.

Intentional Style Selections

When a team can clearly picture their target audience's tastes, preferences, worries, and issues, they more easily discern which forms of communication will reach that audience. The team should carefully explore issues such as whether to have a choir and which instrumentation or other art forms would most effectively accomplish your goals. In Willow Creek's early years, we decided our nonchurched friends would respond best to contemporary music, drama sketches, and multimedia presentations. These were not arbitrary choices based simply on our own preferences—although we enjoyed those creative mediums as well. The friends we hoped to invite on a spiritual journey with us were the people we sought to understand and appeal to with our communication style.

I cannot emphasize enough that the best creative planning comes from team members who themselves are building at least a few significant friendships with people in the target audience—people whom they genuinely care about and pray for regularly. When we have such friendships, we look at all decisions about planning services through those lenses. Most of my nonchurched friends are parents I have met through my daughters' athletic teams. When I participate in creative planning for our services, I always think about whether the ideas we kick around would reach these friends I have grown to love. If you are essentially planning a worship service for believers, you should have them uppermost in your mind as you shape style and content for those hours.

By far the biggest artistic decisions begin with music. Nothing causes more conflict in a church than opinions about music styles. This has been going on for centuries and will probably be the case until the end of time! We have all heard complaints that the music is out of date or too edgy, too loud or too boring. People of all ages feel passionate about music, because it holds deep, personal meaning. All of us associate specific life memories with certain kinds and pieces of music. For all generations—and especially young people—music is the language by which we process our deepest thoughts and feelings. There are also strong preferences regarding country-western, classical, adult contemporary, alternative, hip-hop, or big band. No wonder there are radio stations for every conceivable audience.

So what happens when...

this group of people with diverse tastes and passions about music all show up to the

same service on Sunday morning? It's a recipe for disaster. Some music directors

simply rotate styles, trying to keep everyone happy some of the time. Others land on

one style and hope people will somehow adjust. Some churches offer different venues,

each with its own worship style, and then project a video message so all attenders

hear the pastor at the same time. Still another option is to create many different

services to appeal to different audiences.

I know of one Chinese Christian church that offers seven unique services every Sunday, with the doors finally closing at 3:30 P.M.!

The challenge is to find the musical style and range best suited to your target audience. You can then occasionally stretch the audience by including a niche slightly outside that range. These judgment calls are exceedingly complex as each church tries to find its way. In planning our mid-week worship service, we've learned we can offer a wider range of musical styles *if we continually teach our believers about the importance of tolerance and grace.* We'd rather do this than encourage selfish consumers who are only happy with their preferred worship style.

Music styles change more quickly than just about anything in our culture. Recently, our high school ministry was selecting music for a gathering in September. One team member proposed a song, but others in the group disagreed, claiming, "That song was so 'summer'!" Worship planners must discern when to temporarily retire a "tired" song and when to resurrect a historic hymn or chorus that might breathe meaning and new life into our worship. It is important to keep listening to those we aim to reach and experimenting until we find an effective range of music styles.

We need to carefully select other art forms, too, asking:

- What visual environment will reach this audience? What do we want people to see?
- What art forms—video, dance, visual arts, etc.—are in our toolbox? What art forms should we develop to more effectively deliver God's truth?
- Given our goals and audience, how interactive should the service be? How much do we want attenders to actually do or experience? Should we take an experiential or presentational approach?

I love the passionate, focused dialog that planning teams have when each person truly gets the mission and audience. We can move from conversations based only on our personal preferences to meaningful exchanges based on what God has led us to do together. We ask, "Did our content choices effectively reach our target audience?" not, "Did our most influential donor, the chairman of the elders, or our own spouse like the service?"

No matter what we plan, attenders will give feedback in person, on the phone, or through the mail—sometimes with unbelievable intensity! But we must have a strong center to graciously respond, without losing our way in what God has called us to do. Otherwise we are in danger of falling into what John Ortberg describes as "easily drifting from mission to complaint management." In other words, not all feedback should be weighed equally.

When we receive a note or point of view from someone who does not understand or agree with our mission, we respond lovingly without deciding to change course. However, when we hear from someone who has a stranglehold on our service goals or from a person in the center of the target audience, we pay extremely close attention and take action. We need to remain strong in our intentions and true to our callings, rather than vacillate according to the latest complaints or congregational poll. If you are designing services for seekers, remember that believers' voices will always be much louder, because seekers rarely have anyone who speaks on their behalf. The team entrusted with planning weekly services must be unified in their commitment to select content according to mission.

Intentional Casting

One other dimension of good planning involves the *who*—selecting those people who will deliver the material you have so carefully prepared. We call this *casting*. Communication experts agree it really matters, which is why certain television news anchors and movie stars earn exorbitant amounts to bring in an audience. Listeners profoundly react to the person delivering the content, no matter how powerful that content—a song, drama sketch, or spoken message—is. I urge you to make careful casting decisions, even on a small team with limited options. When we began Willow Creek, we had one pastor who could teach messages; three drama volunteers, none of whom had previous theater training; and a small team of vocalists and instrumentalists.

We did not have a host of options. But no matter what size your church or volunteer teams, take care when asking someone to play a vital role in the service. Aim to cast those who are normal, authentic, and prepared.

- **Normal**. This sounds so goofy, but all too often attenders perceive that people up front do not sound, dress, or act normal. We want to cast people that attenders can easily relate to. Service leaders shouldn't change their voices or use churchy or unnaturally religious lingo. They should dress appropriately for the culture, not calling too much attention to themselves but fitting in with the majority of those in the room. If a pastor or vocalist dresses far more formally than anyone in the congregation, audiences feel awkward and distant.

- **Authentic**. People in the seats need to believe the men and women on the platform are for real—that they struggle like anyone else, but also that they genuinely seek to live out the truths they espouse. If attenders perceive that those up front are fake, pretentious, or simplistic about life's complexities, they'll tune out. But when someone on the platform connects well with the congregation and is trusted, communication can be greatly enhanced.

- **Prepared**. An audience gets extremely nervous if they sense a person on the platform is nervous, lost, or unprepared. It's impossible to relax and receive truth if you are worried that the person up front will fall apart! Give rookies time to build confidence with small roles or during less-pressured weeks. Do not cast a rookie in a major role for a key service or event.

Churches fortunate to have more than one teaching pastor face different casting issues. For example, we've learned that our congregation needs and expects to hear from our senior pastor and a few other team members for major holidays like Christmas, Good Friday, and Easter. That's when we schedule team members who have the strongest connection and history with our people. Smaller churches should make sure their pastor and core team do not take

2	23	24	25	26	27	28
FIRST DAY OF WINTER	help with stage setup	Christmas Eve Services AII TEAM ONBOARD	CHRISTMAS DAY Vacation			
am elder meeting	10am meeting					
9	30	31	1	2	3	4
		NEW YEAR'S EVE				

personal vacations during significant ministry seasons. In times of crisis for your church or in your nation, this same team will be needed to minister to a hurting congregation. We saw this with tremendous clarity in the Sundays following the tragedy of September 11. Our people desperately needed to hear from team members and pastors they trusted.

Finally, the people up front should represent the target audience's general age range and cultural traits. To effectively bridge the racial divide, you absolutely must cast people who represent the racial diversity you hope to see in attendance. None of us wants to attend a church where no one up front is like us. We relate best to those whose lives seem similar to the ones we lead Monday through Saturday.

Planning vs. Spontaneity

Does this intense planning focus leave room for the Holy Spirit to move spontaneously, surprising everyone with a sense that God had another plan? Yes! It's true that careful planning risks squeezing out supernatural, unpredicted times when our Creator reveals his presence and fills us with wonder. But it's entirely possible to plan worship services and seeker events that leave room for God to act. It is crucial not to miss what God might be up to in the moment. So how does this tension between planning and spontaneity get played out in the real world of the hour on Sunday?

Don't assume that service elements planned a month in advance are somehow less spiritual than moments that occur spontaneously. Our God is as fully capable of flowing his power to artists and teachers a few weeks in advance as he is able to do so in the moment. It's mistaken to believe that planning automatically gets in the way of what God might want to do. I truly believe our heavenly Father expects us to discipline ourselves, listening for his voice all along the way—from early brainstorming to the actual minutes of the Sunday service. Many service ideas conceived in advance are clearly anointed and touch the congregation with true spiritual power.

The best strategy combines careful planning with openness and flexibility to change that plan as God might lead. For example, our worship leaders come to our mid-week service with a well-thought-out and carefully rehearsed worship order. Yet we trust them to discern throughout worship if the Spirit is prompting any adjustments. Perhaps a time of silence suddenly feels most worshipful. Maybe singing an unplanned song most effectively responds to what is happening in the moment. The worship leader may also decide not to do a song or to stop and simply pray with the congregation as God leads. In many churches, a pastor will step forward and lead the congregation with some spiritual direction that was not previously planned, but flows out of response to the Spirit. These choices should be entrusted to leaders who have earned trust from both the leadership team and the congregation.

We're also learning how to make room for more spontaneity in our seeker services. When our pastor or another godly leader guides us in reflection or spiritual direction, they need freedom to read the room and make adjustments based on what is happening in the hearts of people. We do not want to miss out on anything our God might have in mind. If attenders sense that every part of the service goes like clockwork, with total precision and nothing unexpected, the service can begin to feel over-produced and somewhat cold. I urge all planning teams to balance the service planning responsibility with leaving room for God's surprises outside or in addition to those plans.

The Holy Adventure

Sometimes I admit my daily life feels like an endless series of planning meetings. My mother often quips that my tombstone will simply state, "Gone to another meeting!" But there's a huge payoff for carefully planning church services. I see it whenever a service ends and I can sense that our ideas actually connected, that people had a rare opportunity to sense the presence of our loving God, and that they are not heading out to their cars quite the same as when they came in. How do I know this? It is not easy to quantify or substantiate. I hear it in enthusiastic voices in the lobby. I see it in the eyes of a friend I have brought, or better yet, in their words. Maybe most telling of all, I see people coming back Sunday after

NANCY BEACH

"GONE TO ANOTHER MEETING"

Sunday, and I know that does not happen unless it has proven to be worth their time.

This past weekend, we invited a guest worship leader from Ireland to share his music with our congregation. During the entire hour, our people truly sensed God's powerful presence. At the end of the service, our guest led the people in a beautiful song, enhanced by a choir and excellent Celtic-style band. After our pastor closed the service in prayer, the Irish worship leader simply reprised the song, intending to play as the congregation left the room. But almost nobody made their way to the exits. They just kept singing and singing, pouring out their hearts and wanting to linger as long as possible. A friend of mine was stunned to discover his eight-year-old son, down on his knees, because he was deeply affected by the song. I love it when people are so enriched by their time in church that they don't want to leave.

EVERY MINUTE

you and I spend wrestling to understand our mission, getting to know our audience, and sifting through a myriad of creative ideas and possibilities **IS WORTH IT WHEN** we know that God has moved in the hearts of real people. As long as I live, I will never get over what a glorious, holy adventure **WE ENGAGE** in as we plan the hour on Sunday and partner **WITH OUR HEAVENLY FATHER!**

Questions to Explore

1. Evaluate your church's attention to selecting series or topics for recent weekend services. What grade would you give yourselves for intentional creativity and for discerning topics relevant to your attenders?

2. Name a recent series that worked just right at a certain time of the year. Can you remember one that might have worked better during a different season?

3. Examine whether your church's style selections and service designs are based on your mission and target audience. If you could start over today and had permission to change anything, what might you do differently?

4. Assess your balance between careful advance planning and allowing room for spontaneity. Do you lean too far in either direction? What adjustments might God lead you to make?

chapter **four**

I know
two things
for sure:
artists
are not
easy to
lead;
and artists
desperately
need
leadership.

Leadership
WILL SOMEONE PLEASE POINT THE WAY?

What first comes to mind when you hear the word *artist*? I have asked this question in workshops I teach all around the world. Regardless of location, the responses I receive are remarkably consistent and fall into two categories—one negative, one positive:

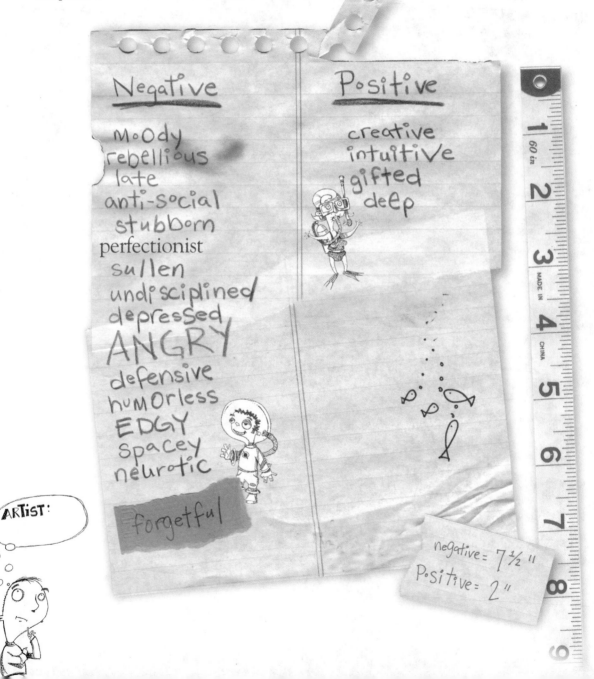

Negative
- moody
- rebellious
- late
- anti-social
- stubborn
- perfectionist
- sullen
- undisciplined
- depressed
- ANGRY
- defensive
- humOrless
- EDGY
- spacey
- neurotic
- forgetful

Positive
- creative
- intuitive
- gifted
- deep

ARTiST:

negative = 7½"
Positive = 2"

As you can see, one list is **much longer than the other!** While most of us deeply appreciate what artists bring to the world and to our churches, we also carry many negative impressions of artists. We base these impressions partly on experience, partly on what we've read and seen in the media. Although it's dangerous to generalize about any group of people, many stereotypes have at least some basis in truth, including some negative stereotypes about artists.

I love artists. I always have. I cannot imagine a world without the beauty, perspective, and sheer joy artists bring. Where would any of us be if our planet were void of music, poetry, dance, paintings, literature, and film? Our lives would lack color and fullness and the human understanding that comes with telling stories through images, movement, and words. The most powerful moments and significant memories in the life of our church have been created by our artists! I use the term *artists* for those who create videos, design the stage, dance, write, sing, paint, play an instrument, mix the sound, and contribute overall ideas. *They're all artists.*

Those who provide leadership to arts ministries have two primary goals: to lead artists in creating meaningful moments in church and to lead artists to become more like Jesus. Providing leadership to artists isn't just about what takes place up front in a service; it's every bit as much about what goes on in the hearts and lives of the artists themselves. This two-fold goal is a huge challenge. After three decades in arts ministry, I know two things for sure: artists are not easy to lead; and artists desperately need leadership.

Artists Are Not Easy to Lead

My husband serves as a volunteer leader in two ministry areas generally filled with left-brained, thinker-type people. He often accomplishes kingdom work by going to meetings, making decisions, and then following through with a list of tasks. This always strikes me as rather simple and uncomplicated compared with the group of people I get to lead. Artists have great strengths—and extremely complicated weaknesses. It's part of how God created them. They feel things deeply and therefore can craft moments that tap into what others feel but can't seem to express. Yet this very strength—feeling things deeply—can drive artists to self-doubt, perfectionism, and fear of failure.

As I scroll through the names of favorite Willow Creek artists, I can hardly think of a person who easily processes emotions or who hasn't traveled a somewhat tortuous journey toward freedom and joy. One favorite artist will always hurt because her father abandoned her; a musician on our team deals with periodic depression; yet another always fights voices from his past that scream his work will never measure up to his own standards. Frankly, leading these folks is a huge challenge.

Artists have the ability to see and give expression to things others don't. They don't readily accept the status quo, and others sometimes perceive artists' unique perspectives as bucking the system. Single-mindedly devoted to their craft, artists often slip into self-absorption and lose sight of the big picture. It's rare to have a simple conversation with artists or a simple decision about approach and ministry. Artists often see the world in shades of gray rather than

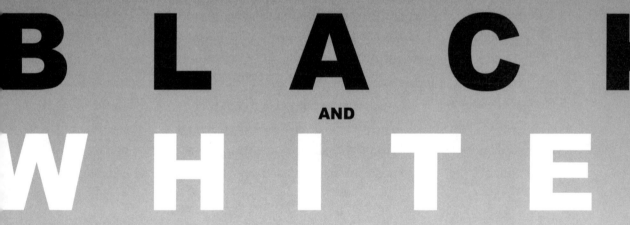

BLACK

AND

WHITE

and they resist quick or simplistic conclusions.

I experience the challenge of working with artists most vividly when we meet with our pastors to discuss drama scripts. Recently we wrestled to discern the take-home message of a Good Friday script. The writer and drama directors fought for the artistic integrity of the piece itself. The pastors sought to protect the audience from ambiguity, while the artists defended subtlety. What a delicate dance! If those who lead artists attempt to be authoritative, handing down edicts and expecting the team to *just do it*, turmoil and trouble result.

Artists Desperately Need Leadership

Artists require effective, godly leadership as much or more than any other group in the church. Without a doubt, gifted artists are treasures to any ministry, because they bring what no one else can bring. The sad truth is that, like all Christ-followers, artists can easily lose their way. They get distracted or discouraged. Countless Christian artists have fallen to sins of pride, greed, jealousy, perfectionism, bitterness, despair, or sexual sin. We've all heard stories of those who have lost their credibility and ended up out of ministry altogether. Each story is tragic, a loss for the artist's own soul and family as well as to the kingdom here on earth. It's not necessarily true that artists sin more than other Christians do, but their circumstances and temperaments pose unique challenges. I wish I could say our church has been exempt from such losses, but that is not the case. Some of our artists—including a woman I'll call Melanie—have lost their way, causing tremendous sadness and loss on our team.

Melanie was one of our most gifted and beloved vocalists. She communicated music with passion, skill, and sensitivity. Although she had two young children at home, Melanie volunteered many hours for rehearsals, services, and community out-reach events. Eventually, I invited Melanie to join a small group of women from our ministry who met weekly at my house. Over time we learned that Melanie had a troubled marriage and was in counseling. I began to discern that Melanie's devotion to ministry was—not all, but in part—an escape from her challenges at home.

But I failed to see just how serious the marital issues were. I hoped that the counseling would help Melanie and her husband sort out their problems and eventually all would be well. Then the plot began to clot. One of our male volunteer instrumentalists, also married, became very friendly with Melanie. They had great chemistry and spent time together at our long rehearsals and multiple services. Naively, I thought this was an innocent, healthy, male-female friendship. Given our ministry pace and my many duties, I didn't pay close attention to what was really going on. You know where this is going. . . .

Their brief affair ended two marriages and caused both individuals to lose their ministries. I learned how vulnerable artists can be when they share the exhilaration of using their art in meaningful church work, spend long hours together, and are tempted to compromise. I'll never forget the night Melanie stood before our music team to confess her sin and explain that she would be taking a long leave of absence to seek restoration. I vacillated between sadness and anger at myself. How could I have missed this? She was in my own small group, for crying out loud! I felt like an incredible failure as a leader and as a friend.

Moral failures are the most public but aren't the only way Christian artists end up in the ditch. Many artists are derailed not by their own failings so much as a lack of vision or encouragement from their leaders. Without consistent reminders and affirmation, artists lose sight of why they serve and often give up trying to use their gift for God. Some invest their talents in the secular world, where they feel a greater sense of freedom. Other artists conclude that church leaders don't really understand how hard it is for them to prepare for services, give so vulnerably from their hearts, and still have a healthy life outside of ministry. As a result, they often feel used and unappreciated. For all these reasons and more, artists need leaders who move toward them and lead them with diligence. We can all get better at leading artists, and the kingdom will flourish as we do. The best place to start is by growing in our understanding of artists.

Understanding Artists

The more we understand artists, the more we will love them and know how to effectively lead them. How hard it is for us to understand artists depends on how artistic we consider ourselves to be. I have a mixture of artistic and leadership gifts that makes me feel fairly comfortable in two worlds—the world of true artists and the world of more left-brained thinker types. But because I do not consider my own temperament to be like that of a pure artist, I explore and learn more about artists'

SELF PORTRAIT OF MARK DEMEL BY MARK DEMEL

experiences and

emotional make-ups by listening to and reading about them.

MARK'S DOODLES

My friend and team member Mark Demel is one of my favorite artists.
God poured out his abundant grace when Mark met Jesus as a young adult and
then began to discover the gifts our Creator entrusted to him. Mark was originally
in the insurance business; he also moonlighted from home as a cartoonist. Several
years ago, Mark discovered acting and writing gifts and has since acted in and/or written some of our most moving dramatic presentations. I love trying to figure out what
Mark is thinking during our creative meetings—his intuitive mind is a wonder to
behold. Usually it's impossible for Mark to sit still as we wrestle with ideas. This visual
thinker jumps up to doodle concepts and possibilities on a flipchart.

One day I asked Mark if I could stop by and see the home studio where he does
illustrations. Experiencing Mark in that environment provided a window for me to
understand him better. I saw the immaculate space he created for design, his need for a
view of the neighborhood outside this quiet room upstairs, removed from his young
children's exuberance.

I know that the process of how we go about our ministry matters enormously to
Mark—and too much of the time we don't get that process quite right. Mark flourishes
in an environment where we have at least some freedom to risk and even fail. He
delights in heading down apparent rabbit trails of creative options, because he knows
that some of those wild paths may actually bring us to a glorious place, if only we'll be a
little patient. The more I try to figure out who Mark is and how he thinks, the more I
realize how incredibly unique he is. I absolutely believe that leading artists is itself an
art, and in many ways, I am still a rookie.

Reading about artists and how they work has also been extremely valuable to me.
In her wonderful book about the craft of writing, *Bird by Bird,* author Anne Lamott
captures the daily struggle of the creative process with humor and honesty:

'But how?' my students ask. "How do you actually do it?" You sit down, I say. You try to sit d o w n at approximately the same time every day. This is how you train your unconscious to kick in for you creatively. So you sit down at, say, nine every morning, or ten every night. You put a piece of paper in the typewriter, or you turn on your computer and bring up the right file, and then you stare at it for an hour or so. You begin rocking, just a little at first, and then like a huge autistic child. You look at the ceiling, and over at the clock, yawn, and stare at the paper again. Then, with your fingers poised on the keyboard, you squint at an image that is forming in your mind—a scene, a locale, a character, whatever—and you try to quiet your mind so you can hear what that landscape or character has to say above the other voices in your mind. The other voices are banshees and drunken monkeys. They are the voices of anxiety, judgment, doom, guilt. Also, severe hypochondria. There may be a Nurse Ratched-like listing of things that must be done right this moment: foods that must come out of the freezer, appointments that must be canceled or made, hairs that must be tweezed. But you hold an imaginary gun to your head and make yourself stay at the desk. There is a vague pain at the back of your neck. It crosses your mind that you have meningitis. Then the phone rings and you look up at the ceiling with fury, summon every ounce of noblesse oblige, and answer the call politely, with maybe just the merest hint of irritation. The caller asks if you're working, and you say yeah, because you are. Yet somehow in the face of all this, you clear a space for the writing voice, hacking away at the others with machetes, and you begin to compose sentences. You begin to string w-o-r-d-s-t-o-g-e-t-h-e-r like beads to tell a story. You are desperate to communicate, to edify or entertain, to preserve moments of grace or joy or transcendence, to make real or imagined events come alive. But you cannot will this to happen. It is a matter of persistence and faith and hard work. So you might as well just go ahead and

get started."

TRUE TO LIFE

Monkey bu

If you resonated with Anne's words, you are most likely a creative person yourself—if not, seek to benefit from her insights. As one who has been called to lead artists, I want to increasingly celebrate the wonder of how God designed and works through these treasured people. Learning to shepherd and guide artists is more than worth any challenges we will face.

Do~Overs

When I think back over my journey as a leader of artists, I celebrate some parts and deeply regret others. My short list of regrets includes four key areas where I'd love the chance for a *do-over*. If I could start over, I would keep the vision clear, lead *up* more effectively, be realistic about the amount of output, and confront character issues right away.

1. Keep the Vision Clear

Even the most devoted volunteer artists can grow fuzzy about why we are doing what we are doing. We require consistent reinforcement of our vision and our core values. Warren Bennis, a highly respected expert, has written numerous books on leadership. My favorite is *Organizing Genius*, because it focuses on critical ingredients for leading creative teams—what Bennis calls *Great Groups*. After extensive study of many hugely successful organizations, Bennis concluded, "The talented people who make up Great Groups are not easily led. Often the leader's role is simply to keep them pointed in the right direction." It is essential for leaders of artists to err on the side of over-communicating the purpose for serving and the church mission rather than assuming everyone just gets it and will always get it.

Keeping the vision clear becomes exceedingly difficult as volunteer teams grow. Newer team members require orientation to arts ministry expectations, strategy, and values. Veteran servants also need frequent reminders, because, as our pastor often says,

 "**vision leaks.**" With so many rehearsals and services, how do we make time to communicate our foundation?

4

Our team has experimented with many strategies to keep vision clear, such as gathering all arts ministry volunteers a few times each year. We highlight core values and inspire our teams by showing them examples of changed lives. In a recent such gathering, called a *Town Hall Meeting*, I invited a drummer new to our music ministry to tell his story. Wes' description of coming to Willow Creek—feeling blown away by the music, and seeing a drum set on stage just like his at home—was a great inspiration to our team. Wes told us he couldn't get over the quality and style of music he was hearing at a church. Over time, Wes investigated Christianity and volunteered to serve. Eventually he gave his life to Christ. After hearing this real-life story from a member of one of our very own teams, our volunteers jumped to their feet in applause. Wes vividly reminded us why we serve.

We expect our team leaders to consistently reinforce both the church vision and our team values through individual conversations and prayer times in smaller rehearsal settings. The production team, for example, often meets backstage before a service, holding hands in a circle of prayer and asking God to work mightily through our ministry. Leaders use e-mail to communicate essential information and showcase stories of those who are living out our core values. Despite all these efforts, keeping the vision clear is a never-ending process.

2. Lead Up Effectively

Artists in every church need a bridge to those who make the major decisions—including the pastor, elders, board of directors, or any other leadership body with influence over the artists. Oh, how I wish I had been a more effective bridge. Leading up involves advocating for what artists need to flourish and clearly communicating to artists and leaders.

For example, very few church boards comprehend why the arts ministry needs certain equipment—and certainly won't believe what some of this equipment costs. All too often I became so absorbed in leading the artists that I neglected to provide the right leaders with vital information about the arts ministry and our part of the church's overall mission. Once again, it is dangerous to assume that others understand if we are silent. Artists also need a fuller picture of all the departments competing for limited church resources. Otherwise they develop **tunnel vision** and ignore other significant ministry areas.

Doug Veenstra has greatly enhanced my leadership horsepower. We co-led our arts ministry until Doug and his family relocated. As partners, Doug and I focused on what we do best. I concentrated on overall creative direction for services and events; Doug developed and led our people day to day. I wasn't aware how poorly I led *up* until I watched Doug do it so masterfully. He carefully built relationships with a few members of our church board and the elders and also communicated frequently with key leaders in other departments. Doug painted a picture of our team's challenges, limited resources, and need to keep the stress in check. Somehow he maintained a positive *can-do* attitude, making sure the other leaders knew our fervent desire to serve God with our gifts as fully as possible.

During the budget process, Doug championed our ministry needs while keeping the overall church vision and other priorities in mind. He was never abrasive or demanding; Doug truly listened to others and then communicated in a clear and compelling way. If you lack such strengths, I urge you to find a volunteer or staff member who can help you play this vital role of leading up. I'll always be looking for someone just like Doug.

3. Be Realistic about Creative Output

I'd love a do-over for how I have led the pacing of our key artists' creative output. To put it bluntly, I have not protected them enough from our excessive pace and potential burnout. Church artists are given both the blessing and the curse of frequent deadlines—every seven days! I have always had enough smarts to know artists are not machines, and there is a limit to how much they can produce with innovation, joy, and health. But discerning exactly where that limit is keeps me learning the hard way.

When I first accepted a leadership role in the arts ministry, we had only one drama writer—a very gifted guy named Judson Poling. Jud was expected to create a new, eight-minute drama sketch every weekend, for about fifty Sundays a year. Even as a novice leader I knew that was ridiculous. Others wondered why Jud's scripts didn't hit a home run every week. This was not about Jud being a slacker or not caring about our services—his creativity had real limits, and he simply was not given adequate breaks to get re-fueled. Once we adjusted Jud's workload and developed a few other writers, he soared as a creative contributor and has continued to craft powerful drama scripts for nearly twenty-five years.

As an artist in the corporate world of Hallmark Cards, Gordon MacKenzie sought to preserve and protect his own creative spirit. *Orbiting the Giant Hairball*, one of my all-time favorite books, beautifully describes Gordon's journey. In one delightful chapter Gordon illustrates the tension between management and artists when it comes to production pace. He asks the reader to imagine a serene pasture where a dairy cow is quietly eating grass, chewing her cud, and swishing her tail. Outside the fence stands "a rotund gentleman in a $700, powder-blue, pinstripe suit." This gentleman is livid that the cow is not working hard. He doesn't understand that whatever milk the cow produces when placed on the milking machine is directly related to the time the cow spends out in the field—"seemingly idle, but, in fact, performing the alchemy of transforming grass into milk." Gordon skillfully compares the rotund gentleman to management leaders all over the country who have no patience for the "quiet time essential to profound creativity."

Too many church leaders don't understand that artists who create services need quiet fueling to do their best work. If we try to hook them up to a constant milking machine fifty weeks a year, we will suffocate their best ideas, possibly damage their souls, and most likely lose them for long-term ministry.

Every artist is unique, with a different capacity for creative output. The key to leading them effectively is to understand their rhythms and provide a pace that allows them to stop their relentless output and restore themselves. At Willow Creek, we've addressed this by recruiting more team members to free up artists for certain periods of time. We also provide a few of our creative people extra time off in the summer to break away from their normal routines and breathe fresh air away from our church. I urge church leaders to be realistic about how much your treasured artists can produce before they start to die inside.

4. Confront Character Issues Immediately

My fourth do-over as a leader of artists stems from a lifelong weakness—the desire to avoid conflict. I have sometimes waited too long to address character issues in our artists' lives. Voices in my head whisper that surely the individual is aware of his or her behavior, or that it's not my place to hold the person accountable, or even that others must be dealing with the matter. The story I told about Melanie, the vocalist, might have played out much differently if I had paid closer attention to my instincts and had the courage to ask questions and speak truth. I wonder what pain might have been prevented for her or others if her path had been turned around sooner.

The good news is that after five years of absence from our community, Melanie was fully restored in her faith as well as in her music ministry. One of our most significant memories as a church took place the night Melanie stood before us and told her story. She asked for our forgiveness, the elders prayed for her, and then we heard Melanie's beautiful voice once again sing a song of surrender to Jesus. I still remember the thunderous applause of our congregation, a signal of grace extended. What a glorious kingdom victory! The evening became a teaching opportunity for all of us to confess our sins and escapist desires early on, before we make tragic choices we will regret. We also re-committed ourselves to live in accountable relationships, invite one another to boldly ask how we are really doing, and recognize that all of us will face temptation.

Leaders, don't ever look the other way when a fellow team member might need you most. Under the Holy Spirit's guidance, discern when it is necessary to move toward your friend and lovingly inquire about a pattern you have seen. This includes times when you observe hints of pride, jealousy, a critical spirit, bitterness, laziness, loose talk, or any other behaviors that do not reflect the character of Jesus Christ. Voices in your head will pull you to believe that it's none of your business and that, most likely, everything is really okay. We also tend to make artists, especially highly gifted ones, the exceptions to standards clearly set forth in Scripture for all believers. The Bible makes no such exception. Artists are first and foremost sons and daughters of God. No doubt it is scary for any of us to engage in these difficult conversations—but our team members' lives and churches' spiritual vitality are at stake.

A Leader of Process

At the end of the day, I believe that *process matters just as much to our Lord as product does.* We'll be held accountable for more than what takes place up front in our services—the entire process is ministry, from lunches with volunteers, brainstorming meetings, and rehearsals all the way through to evaluation. If someone were to pull away the curtain like Toto did in *The Wizard of Oz*, could we be just as confident that our process honors God? Or would we be a little ashamed at what lurks behind the scenes? A huge part of honoring our artists centers on leaders' ongoing analysis of process breakdowns and required adjustments.

Changes may not need to be drastic. For years, we rehearsed our services on Saturday afternoons in pieces with the technical teams—drama first, then music, but not in a flow from beginning to end. We thought this was honoring our volunteers by not requiring all of them to show up at once and have too much time waiting around for their part. But both the production teams and the on-stage participants began saying they were frustrated about not having a sense of the overall progression of the service until we did the first one. They expressed a need to walk through the actual transitions and experience the flow themselves in order to do their jobs more effectively and confidently. We learned that these volunteers would prefer to come earlier in exchange for doing the service in order. So we made the change. The process honored their requests and made the entire rehearsal experience feel more sane.

Discerning leaders of artistic teams hold loosely the way things are done, always recognize that if there is a better way to do process, we need to be bold enough to make the change.

Use your antennae to discover what isn't working as well as it could. Truly listen to the people who have the most direct sense of the issues. Whenever we adjust a process to improve the overall experience for our artists, they sense that we care for them and want them to enjoy serving as much as possible.

Nancy — you are the most loving leader I have ever followed. You treat all you do with such a loving spirit. The love you showed me in painful times, the loving support you showed me in hard times, the loving challenge when I needed to step up — I've always wanted to follow a loving leader. Thank you for teaching me, believing in me, and loving me. You did such a great job this year! Well done! Here's to rest and family and refilling for you this summer —

Bruce

Leading with Love

A few years ago, the core of our leadership team was given the gift of a weekend together in New York City. We refueled ourselves with incredible Broadway shows, and we reconnected with one another as we laughed and shared our lives in restaurants and on long city walks. On the final afternoon, I gave each person a set of New York postcards—one for each team member. We took time to thoughtfully write a brief message of affirmation to the other team members, one per card. We sat in a small city park on cold gray benches among the pigeons, reading aloud what we had written for one another, and then giving the cards as a gift to take home. I still have my set.

Bruce Smith, a key leader on our team, oversees our technical production and is the driving force behind countless creative endeavors. On my postcard, Bruce wrote, "I've always wanted to follow a loving leader. . . thank you for teaching me, believing in me, and loving me." There are no words he could have written that would have meant more to me.

When all is said and done, artists simply long to be led with love. They want to know that someone attempts to understand how they are wired, what they need to soar, and how hard it can be for them to keep doing creative work. Those of us who lead artists should begin by asking ourselves if we truly love them. That means wanting the best, God's best, for them.

Whenever we begin to show signs of resenting artists or wishing they could just fly straight and get with the program, we must ask our heavenly Creator to refresh and renew our genuine love for these treasured people. He will enable us to see them as he sees them and to love them with growing depth and joy. One of the most effective ways I know to express our love for artists is to offer them the gift of community—and that is what we'll explore next.

Questions to Explore

1. What adjectives immediately come to mind when you think of artists? Assess your attitudes toward those with artistic gifts and temperaments.

2. What step could you take to more fully understand artists—even if you are one? What book could you read or relationship could you cultivate that would increase your personal appreciation and understanding of artists? (Consider spending an hour with an artist to learn more about his or her process.)

3. How clear is your ministry vision and strategy for the artists on your team, and what can you do as a leader to prevent that vision from becoming fuzzy? Ask five people on your team to write down what they think about the clarity of your vision and strategy.

4. Evaluate your effectiveness at leading up. How can you be a stronger advocate for your artists with the key decision makers in your church? If you are not the leader, are there ways you could help in this process?

5. Think of your most creative people. How realistic are your creative output expectations for each individual? What can you do to prevent burnout and preserve the contributions and health of these priceless people? If you aren't the leader, what can you do to more clearly express your capacity and limits?

6. Did the Holy Spirit bring anyone from your team to mind as you read about confronting character issues? If so, prayerfully discern if you need to move toward the one whose behaviors concern you.

7. Evaluate accountability in your arts ministry culture. How can you create an environment where artists are held accountable in love for their character? Be honest about any areas where you may have allowed artists to be the exception to scriptural guidelines, and commit to going after those areas.

chapter **five**

When
it's all
said and
done,
I want
to cross
the
finish line
knowing
that I
was a
part of
a team
who loved
one another
outrageously
and did
ministry
side by side
until the
end.

It was a Tuesday night, and I was cleaning up the dishes after supper, weary from a long day of meetings and looking forward to a little downtime after getting the children to bed. My husband was out for the evening, and my young daughters were playing in the family room when the phone call came. With a shaky voice and broken heart, our drama director, Steve Pederson, reported tragic news. One of his drama team volunteers had just lost a five-year-old daughter in a car accident, and his wife lay seriously injured in the hospital. A drunk driver changed their lives forever. I asked Steve what hospital he was calling from and told him I'd get there as soon as I could. After arranging for someone to come care for my girls, I hurried to support the Tomassi family and Steve. I will never forget the anguish in the voice of the father, Randy, as he fell into my arms, sobbing that his precious daughter Gracie was gone.

The rest of that night was a display of love and support unlike anything that hospital had ever seen. Gradually, almost every member of the drama team learned about the tragedy and made their way to be with Randy. They cried with him, prayed for Randy's wife, Terry, and lingered until the nurses insisted it was time to go home. But that was truly only the beginning of their amazing support and love.

In the next days, weeks, and months, that team of drama volunteers provided practical compassion for this hurting family, displaying the outworkings of genuine Christian community. Team members prepared meals, arranged childcare for a younger daughter, planned a beautiful memorial service, and made countless visits to listen, to pray, and to encourage. As horrible as the situation was, I rejoiced to see the payoff after years of building authentic community among our artists.

Occasionally, someone will ask me about my most treasured memories of ministry at Willow. The person often assumes I will describe Willow Creek's twentieth anniversary service with 20,000 people at Chicago's United Center or one of our major artistic moments in a Christmas or Easter service. While those memories do mean a lot to me, what first comes to mind are much smaller moments, moments of connection with a group of artists who have become more than just fellow servants—they are also my friends.

I remember moments when we've laughed together so hard my stomach ached and moments when we've wept over another's pain as we gathered in a circle to pray. I picture washing one another's feet on the back deck of a house in Wisconsin. I remember attending a Broadway play that moved us so deeply none of us left until the ushers kicked us out. We de-briefed that experience as a team and shared what was going on inside our souls. I remember dancing with joy at the wedding of one team member's daughter and standing quietly at the graveside of another team member's father, while the bagpipes played. When it comes right down to it, the memories I treasure most are my memories of community.

The Choice for Community

Leaders of arts ministries, along with their team members, have a decision to make. We can decide to build a community of artists *or* we can decide to merely assemble a team to accomplish a ministry task. I have seen churches make either one of these choices. This choice will directly impact how we do ministry and lead those under our care. It is certainly a legitimate choice to assemble and inspire a team of artists, determining that their needs for community will be met primarily through another branch of the church. In this model, artists are expected to get along with one another, to serve together in unity and joy, but not necessarily to build their strongest ministry relationships with one another.

My own choice has been to build a team of artists who not only serve together, but who also live in authentic community, being known and loved by a few other artists on that team. This choice is far more difficult, but in the end, far more rewarding. Intentionally building a community of artists requires structuring our teams in such a way that there is time for relationships as well as time for rehearsals and services. Community does not just happen—we must decide to make it a core value and then lead our ministries toward that goal.

No matter what option we choose, we cannot ignore our God-given longings for community—every human being has them. Even the people who may seem most introverted or disinterested in connection are designed to know and be known, to love and be loved, to serve and be served, to celebrate and be celebrated. I learned this truth when my husband led a team of volunteers years ago in another ministry.

Like Warren, the other team members were highly task-oriented, quiet folks. They met in our living room, and Warren typically began meetings by diving right into the agenda and diligently working them hard for the next two hours. But gradually, this group of business people started to slip in bits of information about their families and work lives. Soon they were hanging around after the meeting, drinking coffee and sharing

with one another. My husband was not prepared for this turn of events and lamented, "These people want to talk about stuff other than ministry, and pray for each other, and become more like friends, and eat dessert, and maybe not even finish our agenda. This is not what I had in mind!" Eventually, he quit fighting it and helped that team build significant, long-lasting relationships.

Using their ministry gifts helps fulfill volunteers, but loving, joyful, deep friendships within the church make them stay for the long haul. If these valuable servants show up to serve week after week with no sense that anyone else truly knows what goes on in their lives from Monday through

Saturday, they feel empty and, often, used and unappreciated. I can't emphasize enough that building community among several teams is the best way I know to establish a more stable ministry, one that isn't perpetually plagued by a revolving door.

How high is your commitment to creating a culture for artists where significant relationships are not only possible, but encouraged and even expected? If we choose this path, we must be aware that there is a cost. True community doesn't come easily or cheaply.

The Cost of Community

I experienced a season of ministry when I won-dered whether the price of living in community was really worth it. Our department was being restructured, and a consultant came in to help us sort it out. He brought a skilled sensitivity and grace to all our conversations and acted as an advocate for me and every other member on our team. While figuring out what needed to change, I began to feel a lack of support from some friends and coworkers. I didn't believe the best, as

community-shamunity!

1 Corinthians 13 challenges us to do, and I allowed myself to imagine that people I had served and led for so long were turning against me or speaking behind my back. I remember walking out to my car in the church parking lot one day and muttering to myself, "Community-shamunity!"

The Holy Spirit would not allow me to live for long with misery and resentment. That weekend I initiated conversations with those from whom I felt distanced. Through tears I expressed what I was imagining and checked to see what was true and what was from the Evil One. In return, I received nothing but love, grace, and honesty. By coming out of hiding, I experienced the healing of mutual forgiveness and the com-mitment to stay devoted and above board with one another. I decided once again to choose community, even when it gets hard and painful. Withdrawal promises some safety but also means missing out on countless times of joy and support from friends. This simply is not an option I'm willing to choose. But I know I will undoubtedly have other moments down the road when community-shamunity is what I truly feel.

Recognizing the cost, I hope you still share a commitment to building community. Now it's time to move from vision to action. How do we actually live out this value? We'll focus on key elements of community: crafting a structure, taking time to celebrate, and resolving relational conflict.

Crafting a Structure for Community

Artists can develop some level of relationship "through the cracks" of rehearsals and services, but fostering genuine, consistent community requires a small group structure or network. Once a team grows beyond a few people, it becomes impossible for every artist to be significantly connected to all the others. We have to decide how and when to schedule relational time. We've found this to be exceedingly difficult. Our volunteers already sacrifice more hours in ministry than almost any other servants in our church. They regularly show up for rehearsals and services. When we decided to create a small group structure, we intuitively knew it needed to be custom-designed for our unique group.

We began by asking how we could build on times artists were already at church, rather than adding an extra night to already full lives. We grouped artists with others who served in similar areas—production people, instrumentalists, vocalists, drama team members, dancers, etc. Then we considered when each group could gather around existing rehearsal or service times. For example, some instrumental small groups decided to meet between our two Sunday morning services, because they were already hanging around together during that window of time. Technical teams decided to gather before they set up on Saturday afternoons. Vocal and drama small groups made time on selected Tuesday nights before or after rehearsals. We had to be realistic about the frequency of meetings—most of them don't come together every week.

Group size is key. Keep groups small to allow maximum opportunity for connection and support. We like to have between five and eight in a group. A volunteer, who is

coached and supported by another leader as needed, leads each group. In most cases, spouses are not included in the groups only because meeting times are connected to serving times. We do offer a few couples groups for those who prefer that option.

Experiment with a structure until you find one that works best for your unique situation and church. There isn't just one right way to craft community, and all of us must discern how God is leading our own teams. We've also wrestled with what should optimally happen in these groups, because the options are unlimited. Should group meetings be Bible study times, prayer gatherings, sharing marathons, or what? Although we continually experiment with what is realistic and most important, we believe all groups should strive to provide care and connection, accountability and spiritual formation.

Care and Connection

No matter what size your church, every individual needs to feel that there is a small group of people who truly know what's going on in their lives and who will support them when needed. We all want someone to know if we're struggling at work or got a promotion, if our dog is sick or if one of our kids scored a soccer goal. It takes time for everyone in a small group to update each other on their lives. Sometimes we launch this time of connection by asking, "What were your   and   points this past week?" or "How can we specifically be praying for you?" Ideally, each person needs to know he or she will have a moment to be heard. If the entire group time is devoted to a curriculum or Bible study, with no time to share our lives, then most individuals won't leave feeling any more known or understood than when they walked in.

5

We also need to know without a doubt that this small group will show up when we most need their help. If this is not to be a group of fellow artists, it needs to be another clearly identified group within the church. When my daughter Johanna was two years old, she came down with a mysterious high fever that wouldn't go away, and ended up in the hospital for five days. My husband was unavoidably out of town for part of that time, attending a funeral. I'll never forget all the support I received as I sat at Jo's bedside—all my small group friends came to listen, provide practical help, and simply be with me. I was deeply grateful for community that week. I want every volunteer on our artistic teams to know that when any storm of life assaults them, they won't have to carry the burden alone. We teach our volunteers that when it comes to funerals, hospital stays, new babies, a flood, or a fire—**just show up!**

Accountability and Spiritual Formation

At Willow we firmly believe that true life-change happens most often in the context of small groups. It's in community that we seek to apply challenges from the pulpit and from personal times with God. If Jesus Christ is to be formed more fully in each one of us, we need people who know us well to hold up a loving mirror. The purpose of gathering in groups is not simply to add more knowledge to our already full brains—it's much more about learning how to live out our beliefs. Time with our little communities should ultimately result in men and women who are more loving, kind, patient, generous, truthful, humble, and devoted to Christ this month than we were last month. Otherwise, why are we coming together?

In the early years of building our church, we failed miserably at holding one another accountable and taking responsibility to help "form Christ" in one another. We were so overwhelmed by dealing with crowds at church and starting new ministries that we lost sight of our responsibility as brothers and sisters in Christ. We stopped asking, "How are you really doing?" or "Are you working too much here at the church with a new baby at home?"

Partly because we looked the other way, some core team members made sinful choices that led to the breakup of marriages and the loss of ministry integrity. We refer to those years as Willow's "train wreck era." I personally experienced the deep pain of seeing

friends I treasured leave our church, fracturing the community I thought would never be broken. The lessons we learned have served us well—we are deeply committed to creating a culture of accountability and growth in Christ-like character. We now recognize that asking difficult questions, not allowing one another to hide, shows deep care. Team prayers—both during rehearsals and before services—are vitally important to cement community and remind one another of what we are all about. When we come before the Lord, offering our gifts to him in the context of community, his Holy Spirit unites us, and we head out to serve with a more godly perspective. Making time for these moments of group prayer adds extra minutes to our rehearsals—but the upside is more than worth it.

Carve Out Time to Celebrate!

On my office bookshelf is a gold figurine that at first glance looks exactly like an Oscar. I didn't receive it at the yearly Hollywood extravaganza; it was given to me in a Wisconsin lodge by a team member wearing blue jeans. But that little statue is as meaningful to me as the ones gathering dust on Meryl Streep's mantle—and even more treasured are the words of affirmation spoken to me that night.

Our team frequently takes time to honor one another and look back at wonderful moments God helped us create. We don't believe we're supposed to wait until we all get to heaven to enjoy our ministry's video highlights together. So, periodically we set aside an evening to remember, give God thanks, and speak words of encouragement to one another.

We most often celebrate at a retreat, away from church and familiar surroundings. For one evening of our department retreat in Wisconsin, I assigned each team member another to honor during our own version of the Oscars. These creative folks took the assignment quite seriously. The only problem was that their huge desire to give recognition—complete with video highlights—resulted in an evening longer than

NANCY BEACH
BEST PERFORMANCE IN
A LEADING ROLE

the real Oscar ceremony! Inevitably these gatherings lead us to honor our heavenly Father, who gave us the gifts, ideas, and opportunities to make a difference. We often kneel and pay tribute to the Creator.

The children of Israel learned to remember God's faithfulness and to celebrate his goodness with feasts of praise. Consider how often the Psalms writers chose to look back at God's miracles to boost their faith. Psalm 77 begins with an anguished cry to God for help; then the writer changes perspective:

"I will remember the deeds of the LORD; yes, I will remember your miracles of long ago. I will meditate on all your works and consider all your mighty deeds" (Psalm 77:11–12).

Celebrating together also needs to include a whole lot of fun. On our retreats, we make time for play. One January we almost killed one another playing broom hockey on the ice. Many of us forgot we're not eighteen anymore! I fell so hard that the entire team heard my head hit the ice. Miraculously, I was okay and bounced back up to compete. Our team cherishes memories of bowling together to oldies music, tobogganing, tubing on a summer lake, washing dishes in a tiny cottage, and playing serious touch football. It's such a joy to laugh together in a totally different setting.

Taking time to celebrate won't ever seem logical, easy, or economical—but it's more than worth the effort. Give your artists the gift of coming together—to remember and be refreshed by recalling how God has shown his power in your church and on your team. You won't regret it.

Conflict Happens—Handle with Care

When I first began to serve in the arts ministry, I inherited several unresolved conflicts among team members. This led to a series of difficult conversations. I naively thought that once we had worked through these initial conflicts, the rest of my ministry experience would be relatively smooth sailing. Was I ever wrong. I now understand that any ministry is truly a series of difficult conversations. My only explanation is that all of us, including me, are sinners. Put a few fallible humans on a team and, eventually, conflict will erupt. It shouldn't surprise us at all.

I have also observed over the years that perhaps a higher percentage of conflict exists in the arts ministries. Satan must believe he has a phenomenal success rate breeding pride, jealousy, selfishness, and bitterness among the artists in local churches. People at our conference workshops most often ask me how to solve difficulties between team members or between the artists and other church leaders. If your team hasn't yet experienced much conflict, consider yourselves unique and blessed—and don't take it for granted.

Though conflict is inevitable, we can be immensely grateful that Jesus himself taught us how to handle it. In Matthew 18, Jesus clearly prescribes a process for restoring unity among estranged believers. First, if another Christian has wronged us, we are to bring it to their attention, and this exchange should stay "just between the two of you."

Danger, danger, this is where most of us blow it from the start. We fail to go directly to the person we have an issue with and instead share it with a few other people first, often under the guise of asking them for prayer and support. How much pain and unnecessary escalation of tension could be prevented if only we'd obey this first instruction?

DANGER! DANGER! START

COMMUNITY CHEST

STOP SHARING! GO DIRECTLY TO KEVIN.

"then he told me i treat everything like a game!"

"i don't think we should be hearing this!"

If we are approached by a team member who wants to tell us why he's so angry at Kevin, we should immediately stop the conversation and ask, "Have you talked directly to Kevin? I shouldn't be hearing this."

Jesus advised a second guideline only if that first conversation fails to bring peace. Then we are told to take along a third party, someone who can help mediate for the two individuals. Rare cases may require a third phase—bringing the matter before the church (in our case, the elders) for their discernment and help. Countless relational breakdowns would be spared if all believers simply followed Christ's conflict resolution plan. Those of us in leadership must teach and model this process, making it a normal way of doing life in our communities.

Community to the Finish Line

I recently tasted one of the most profound mornings of community I may experience in my entire life. As I mentioned earlier, our original team of Willow Creek founders fractured not long after we began. One founder divorced another team member and eventually moved to another part of the country. That was a devastating era. After all, our team had traveled as teens in rickety buses packed with used sound equipment and guitars, doing concerts in churches all over the Midwest and discovering spiritual gifts and miraculous life change. We grew up together in so many ways. We sang in each other's weddings and held one another's children. We had countless late-night meetings to dream about the church God led us to start with no money, no denomination to support us, no back-up plan, nothing but faith in our Creator and belief in one another. Our bonds were deep and real, and we naively thought they would never be broken.

Through many conversations since our community fractured, most of us have worked through the sadness, pain, and anger. God enabled us to move forward, and almost all of us are still in ministry somewhere. Recently that original founder became very ill. Our pastor arranged for a small group of us who knew him best to get on a seven-seat commuter plane and go see him before it was too late. We really didn't know what to expect. We only knew that we wanted to be in the same room, speak words of love and grace, and somehow bring closure to an acutely painful era. Even the man's ex-wife chose to come, saying she wanted to "finish this thing in community" like we began.

Words can't adequately describe the wonder of what took place in our few hours together. We met in a cold, sterile conference room at a commuter airport with harsh fluorescent lighting and nasty coffee. It was a strange setting for holy moments. One by one, we looked into our friend's eyes, sobered by cancer's ravages. I muffled an audible groan at how his body had changed since we'd last been together. We began as old friends do—reminiscing and laughing about the early 70s, when we all wore certifiably ugly polyester concert outfits in red and white and yellow and white, and thought we knew more than we did about ministry. It felt curiously healing to look back and share our history, one that only a few people would fully understand. Then we took turns letting our friend know how grateful we were for the ways he touched us, for his part in our early adventure.

Our words to him were heartfelt, specific, and deeply honoring. None of us wanted to leave without him knowing for certain what we know—that Willow would never be what it has become without him, and that, in spite of everything, we still love and treasure him. All of the comments were memorable—but it was the moments between former husband and wife that brought to the surface the deepest pain and ultimately the most profound grace. We held our breath as they exchanged words that brought healing to decades of hurt. We cried tears that had been held back too long. And when no more tears would come, we put our friend in a circle, placed hands on his weak body, and offered up prayers for God to be real to him from that day until his final day. Grace flowed that morning, a gift from our merciful God. We drank in the treasure of being together for one last time. *Only in the church* could such an experience have occurred.

When it was time to say good-bye, we knew that thirty years of relating would be reduced to one final embrace. I buried my face against my friend's neck and whispered to him again how much I love him. Then I stood aside, watching as the rest of the group took their turn. When his ex-wife seized her final moments, I thought my heart would burst. Employees in the small airport lobby discerned that something momentous was taking place—one of them handed me a tissue. And then it was time. The security officer buzzed the electric door leading out to the tarmac. We headed out to board our plane, and I couldn't help but turn around for a last look at my precious friend.

On the flight back, though most of us longed for personal space, we sat shoulder to shoulder and knee to knee in the small plane where our sounds of grieving could not be ignored. We didn't speak for a long time. Our commitment to community caused us tremendous pain—but none of us would trade it for anything. I made up my mind in that plane seat to keep paying the price for these close relationships until it's my turn to go to heaven. When it's all said and done, I want to cross the finish line knowing that I was a part of a team who loved one another outrageously and did ministry side by side until the end. I believe with all my heart that's what God intended for every one of his children, and I urge you—no, I challenge you—to make the choice for community.

FINISH LINE

Questions to Explore

1. Carefully assess the commitment of your arts ministry toward intentionally building community. How would you rate yourselves on a scale from 1 to 10 when it comes to making close relationships a priority? Why did you give that rating?

2. Discuss with other team members whether building genuine community is worth the price you will have to pay to make it happen.

3. Take a look at your structure for building community in the arts ministry. What is working well, and what needs improvement? Evaluate whether your meeting schedule, group size, and intentional leadership contribute effectively to achieving this value.

4. If you have arts ministry small groups, rate them on care and connection, accountability and spiritual formation, and taking time to celebrate. Where do you need the most improvement?

5. When conflict erupts in your arts ministry, how closely do you follow the resolution process outlined in Matthew 18? Where does the process most typically break down?

chapter six

When
evaluation
becomes
a normal
way of
life for
local
church
ministries,
everybody
wins, and
the kingdom
advances
step by step,
week by week,
life by life.

Evaluation

HOW DID IT REALLY GO?

I vividly remember the evaluation meetings that Willow Creek's arts ministry held way back in the mid 1970s. Every Monday morning, our boisterous little group would gather around a table in the Marriott hotel restaurant near O'Hare Airport. We sat toward the back, to cause the least amount of distraction to business people seeking a quiet, efficient breakfast. The waitresses knew us too well—and most likely drew straws to see who would have to refill our coffee cups for the next few hours and put up with the paltry tip. We thought we were pretty generous, but nothing we offered could truly compensate for how long we took up space.

Dave Holmbo, the arts ministry founder, led our small group, which included two guys named Rick, one of whom wrote and directed drama. Every week, without fail, he ordered a scrambled egg special with ham called "The All-American Breakfast." He took so many creative gambles with our Sunday dramas, I think, so he needed to play it safe on Mondays with a predictable menu selection. The other Rick was an ex-hippie, a technical genius in sound who also co-created little pieces for the screen we called "medias." His partner, Ginny, a highly gifted illustrator, also attended consistently. I participated as a creative contributor whenever my college schedule would allow. We met at 7:00 A.M.—an hour far too early for most artists to stomach, which partly explains all the caffeine intake and my frequent hikes to the ladies room. Our brand new church paid us little or nothing, so the bills had to be taken care of by other jobs, and meeting early was our only option. Mostly, I remember laughing. Often we laughed so hard I thought the restaurant manager might abruptly ask us to leave. Amazingly enough, we never were kicked out.

We didn't call it an evaluation meeting in those early years—partly because it was so much more. In the very same meeting, we would also be figuring out what to do the next Sunday—just six days later—with only a few creative elements already planned. But somehow Dave instinctively knew that *before moving forward, we needed to look back.* We had no fancy video to watch or official forms to document what we learned. We simply talked it through. How did the hour on Sunday go? Did people respond the way we hoped they would? What worked great that we should celebrate? What did not work that we should resolve to *never ever* do again? Rookies in every way, we were young and willing to take huge risks. We were just making this up as we went along and did not know how to learn except by experimenting. Many of our risks did not pay off, but we stored those experiences in our minds to keep us from treading those creative paths again.

The legacy of evaluation has served our church in profound ways. I am quite certain we would not be the church we are today if individuals and teams hadn't regularly given and received feedback. Such meetings and honest conversations pervade every Willow Creek ministry, from children's ministry to accounting, small groups to building maintenance. Even our teaching pastors ask a few elders, teachers, and selected trustworthy sources to critique their messages.

★ All-American Breakfast ★

Evaluation truly is the only path I know to get better, learn from mistakes, and deposit in our memory banks those holy moments God anointed and used. But sadly, as I talk with church leaders, I often discover that consistent, intentional evaluation meetings are not part of their weekly schedule. And it's not too hard to understand why. The relentless pace of ministry screams at us to just *move on* to the next week. Evaluation requires precious time we don't think we can afford to give. It also seems like water under the bridge—why go over what it is too late now to change? Surely we all know what went well and what did not, so why explore it in more detail? But there are deeper causes for our failure to embrace this core value, causes that require us to look closely at Scripture and our own character flaws.

Is Evaluation Even Biblical or Loving?

The biblical foundation for evaluation is laid from the very first pages of Scripture. In fact, based on the creation account in Genesis 1, my friend John Ortberg states, "God is into feedback." The Bible describes the Creator's process like this: first God creates something—puts the moon in place or gathers the seas—then he steps back, takes a moment, and looks. Throughout the lengthy description of everything God creates, one key phrase is repeated: "And God saw that it was good." Our awesome Creator took time to evaluate and then celebrate what he had crafted before moving on to the next brilliant phase. As human beings made in the image of God, we see this process—creating, stepping back, taking a moment, looking—as an excellent model for our work.

Of course, our desire to engage in feedback is much stronger if all we need to do is celebrate. But since the Fall, men and women have chosen to hide from rather than face the truth about our successes and failures. We all have blind spots and strongly desire to avoid looking at how we miss the mark. When we most need feedback we most often avoid it. This has been true throughout history and is entrenched in our sinful nature.

The Bible clearly teaches that a major difference between the wise and the foolish centers on how we respond to feedback. The foolish consistently shun correction, while the wise seek it out. Consider this description from Proverbs: "If you listen to constructive criticism, you will be at home among the wise. If you reject criticism, you only harm yourself; but if you listen to correction, you grow in understanding" (15:31–32 NLT).

We simply cannot grow as Christians or as artists without learning to receive and embrace feedback. This is a *huge* test of character for anyone serving in ministry. The most natural response is to run as fast as we can from a culture where evaluation is a regular discipline. I am no exception. Right after teaching at a weekend or mid-week service, I step off the platform and join a small circle of friends and coworkers who are waiting to give me feedback on the talk I just gave (and probably sweated through). They usually offer affirmation and only a few suggestions for improvements. But when a section (or more) of my talk does not work as planned, I get constructive truth as well.

One respected coworker frequently tells me that I use too many quotes in my messages, and that I need to declare more often what I believe rather than lean so much into the wisdom of others. I know he is right. But it will never be easy for me to receive this kind of honest feedback. Part of me responds with deep appreciation. But the other part of me—often the bigger part—wonders if the person giving the critical feedback can even begin to understand how hard it is to prepare a message and deliver it *anyway,* and whether, in fact, another church just might welcome my gifts with a little more gratitude!

After I get over my childish thoughts and actually listen and reflect on what I'm hearing, I inevitably discover that the critics truly have my best interests—and the church's best interests—at heart. Giving constructive evaluation to a ministry partner is a most loving way to serve one another. Those who never speak the truth are, in the end, not really in my court, seeking to help me

ARTIST
seeds

Give feedback daily to grow

"some individuals can feel ATTACKED by even the most loving communication of truth."

use my gifts more effectively. My job, and the job of all Christians in local churches, is to learn how to deal with this natural reaction called defensiveness.

Dealing with Defensiveness

I have yet to meet a person whose first, authentic response to constructive criticism is sheer delight. Most people react with knee-jerk defensiveness. In evaluation meetings, some individuals can feel attacked by even the most loving communication of truth. And their behavior makes everyone else in the room feel like they are walking on eggshells during the entire conversation. These highly defensive folks can also launch counter-attacks, questioning the motives and expertise of those who provide the feedback. And when all else fails, they often pull out their ultimate weapon. They spiritualize their decisions or behavior with phrases like "God told me to do this," "The Holy Spirit inspired my song," or "This week's drama script was truly a gift from the Lord." How can anyone counter such authoritative and coercive statements? No matter how long we have been in ministry, it's essential to recognize that we are not the ultimate interpreters of God's ideas or direction. The writer of Proverbs wastes no words describing those who shun feedback—

"It is stupid to hate correction" (Proverbs 12:1 NLT).

Now that's what I call blunt.

Our defensive reactions have deep roots. Feedback makes some of us afraid and anxious. We wonder if being corrected means our place on the team is threatened. Many of us too strongly connect our sense of worth or identity with what we do. We desperately seek approval from the pastor, team, congregation, and even God. Such a performance-driven approach to ministry is tortuous, and laying it aside isn't easy. Our slow transformation involves learning that God will not love us any more than he does right now, no matter what we do. In his powerful little book *Let Your Life Speak*, writer and educator Parker Palmer affirms that identity does not depend on our role, but rather "on the simple fact that we are children of God, valued in and for ourselves." Many of us spend years trying to get that straight.

But beyond fear and approval-seeking, some of us must admit that our defensive-ness comes down to just plain pride. We may secretly think of ourselves more highly than we should and conclude we don't need to change and grow. Like lone rangers

on a quest for ministry independence, we avoid input from anyone who might suggest a change of direction. We must become humble enough to learn from any source and actually seek it out. I have had the awesome privilege of working alongside highly gifted artists and church leaders who display a mature desire to learn and grow from anyone who offers them correction. These unique people stand out for me as heroes.

One shining example is our long-time music director, Rory Noland. As a songwriter and arranger, Rory consistently produces excellent songs and musical scores for our church. Since our earliest days of serving together, Rory has labored over a new piece and then asked a small group for feedback. Several of us (including me) are not even musicians and have nowhere near Rory's skill and experience. But Rory wants to see if the song works for us. He is open to any of our suggestions on how the song could minister more effectively. I remember one such meeting where I loved the new piece, but immediately pointed out a phrase that was not clear to me. Rory graciously accepted my input, but then quietly inquired, **"But did the overall song impact you?"** I learned that day

...ure you get
...g picture.

to first
give
some
big pic-
ture feed-
back before
jumping into
the details. When
Rory or other team
members request
evaluation with such
a gracious spirit, I
have always felt part
of a holy moment,
and I marvel at
their humble ser-
vanthood. They
inspire me to
become more
of a feedback
champion
myself.

Hold our gifts loosely

At Willow Creek and many other churches, we aim to "hold our gifts loosely." Such an attitude grows out of a deep awareness that I did not choose my gifts, and they really don't belong to me. A gracious heavenly Father distributed the gifts, "just as he determines" (1 Corinthians 12), and intends for us to use these gifts to build up the church. My gifts—and yours—actually belong to the local church. As we learn to hold our gifts more loosely, we become far more open to feedback that helps us not only improve our skills and contribute more effectively but also grow closer to one another and advance Christ's cause. **It's not all about me; it's all about the church!** Our response to evaluation will gradually change from fear and defensiveness to authentic gratitude, the more we embrace these radical attitudes. We will rejoice as we see both our own gifts and the work of the kingdom improving and having greater impact.

Let's Get Practical

Acknowledging evaluation's importance and living it out week to week are entirely different things. Because evaluation is a difficult value to sustain and uphold, it is vital to create systems for regular feedback. Unless we intentionally pursue the discipline of evaluation in our communities, our natural avoidance and defensiveness will win the day. I have observed our church and many others pursue this value for over twenty years. The recommendations that follow are based on my experience—and yet I recognize that every local community will need to adapt and determine what works best for them.

I have been surprised to see that periodically we must evaluate our evaluation! We've sometimes recognized that the meeting has become too inefficient, or includes too many people, or hasn't been conducive for feedback. A healthy leader and team will dialogue about how to make the feedback process more effective and then make the necessary changes. What matters is that we keep at it and aim to improve our ministry contributions over time. In the rest of this chapter I will offer a few experience-based principles on the meeting itself, who gets to come, and the path toward creating a safe place for evaluation.

A Scheduled Meeting

Quality evaluation does not occur in hallway conversations, asking "So how do you think Sunday went?" as you pass by. Relentless ministry pace requires carving out a regularly scheduled meeting for effective evaluation. It is usually best to meet within a day or two of the Sunday service, before we forget observations and insights. If the evaluation is part of a meeting that also includes other objectives—such as planning future services—evaluation must be the first item on the agenda or it probably will not happen at all. We must begin by looking back.

I've talked with arts ministry directors all over the world who schedule evaluation meetings at various times and in a wide variety of locations . . . a lunch meeting at a busy Orlando restaurant, an early breakfast at a private home in Frankfurt, a Monday evening gathering for fish and chips at a pub outside of London, a Tuesday morning huddled in a church basement near Detroit, Michigan.

Who Gets to Come

The team leader must carefully select who will be included in the meeting to evaluate Sunday's service. One person can ruin the experience for everyone! Those invited should come expecting that evaluation is part of how we do business. It is not only okay; it is essential to our growth. In considering who to include on an evaluation team, look for individuals who:

- Understand and embrace your church's mission and vision—otherwise discussions will default to one person's opinion versus another person's opinion, which is not constructive.
- Have a vivid picture of your target audience for each service.
- Are committed to the arts ministry team's core values.
- Will strive to communicate with honesty, sensitivity, and love.
- Display humility and lack of self-defensiveness.

Many of us despair, wondering if such people exist on this planet, let alone in our churches. Let me stress that we seek to develop and cultivate team members who increasingly display these traits. We don't expect the group to have all fully arrived. The more a leader can model such godly attitudes, the more others will gradually mature. In fact, it is wise to grow the group slowly, beginning with only three or four participants. Try to keep the evaluation team small enough to allow healthy participation from everyone. Once the meeting grows past eight or ten people, quieter individuals might refrain from speaking up and discussion can become unwieldy.

There are as many combinations of team players for evaluation as there are local churches—definitely not a "one size fits all." Whether or not these men and women serve on your church staff is really not relevant. It is important for the key person responsible for each arts ministry area to be present. This would most likely include the music director, technical director, drama director, etc. In a smaller church, one person probably wears several leadership hats and can represent more than one area. Each church must decide whether the senior pastor or teaching pastor is included in the weekly meeting. At Willow, we receive feedback from our pastors prior to the meeting, usually through our weekend director and a few others who have connected in person or by phone, so we know exactly how he or she reacted to the service. It wouldn't be constructive for our pastors to sit through our intensely detailed evaluations. Yet pastors in some churches join this meeting, and their arts teams can't imagine the process working well without his or her presence.

I highly recommend including perceptive church volunteers in your evaluation. Such individuals may not have played a direct role in carrying out the service, but they can offer a unique perspective from their seat in the congregation or, better yet, from those they invited to join them on Sunday morning. Consider inviting a volunteer to attend occasionally and see how it affects the quality of the dialog.

Creating a Safe Place

Setting the right tone for the evaluation meeting is one of the leader's most daunting tasks. When most artists hear the term *safe place*, they are tempted to laugh because rarely do artists, or any humans for that matter, feel completely safe when we evaluate. Even a group of fully devoted Christian artists is a collection of partially insecure, sensitive, and somewhat frag-ile individuals who have diverse personalities and imper-fect communication skills. Many teams eventually give up on consistent evaluation meetings, because meetings become hurtful or inauthen-tic. But we must not abandon the value just because it's so hard to carry out. To offer con-structive feedback, we need to imagine the atmosphere most likely to promote the sense that we are all in this together, that no one will be attacked, that we'll build an environment bathed in grace. The safe place I picture includes three vital ingre-dients: celebration, trust, and carefully chosen words.

dude, what is happening on the next page? The anticipation is killing me!

Celebration

A few years ago, a visitor from another country quietly observed our weekend evaluation meeting, and we talked privately afterwards. I was sad when she told me that in her church the team members rarely encourage one another for a job well done. Our frequent words of praise for one another made her feel a little uncomfortable, because it was so far removed from her own experience. As I have had the privilege to travel and meet arts teams all over the world, I am often struck by how uncommon it is for teams to celebrate what God is doing through their efforts. I am told that in many cultures, beginning in the home, it is rare for people to praise one another, to acknowledge excellent effort and results. Often artists on church teams tell me they only receive comments when they mess up!

The Bible clearly teaches another, far better way: "And let us consider how we may spur one another on toward love and good deeds, not giving up meeting together, as some are in the habit of doing, but let us encourage one another" (Hebrews 10:24–25). Our praise recognizes the One who distributed our gifts and gave us power and strength to minister. We can certainly speak words of encouragement without forgetting our heavenly Father. I believe it gives God great joy to see his children build one another up. Ministry is exceedingly difficult. Every servant needs to be appreciated and told frequently that his or her contribution matters and has been noticed.

These words of encouragement should be specific and genuine—not just a general phrase like "Great job on Sunday." Artists deeply appreciate it when others observe the nuances of their work and speak to those details. Watch a musician's eyes shine when you tell him you especially liked the creative arrangement leading into a song's chorus. Tell the lighting designer that you noticed how she faded the lights with just the right timing on a powerful drama sketch. See how the sound engineer reacts when you celebrate his mix on a complicated instrumental piece. Such words are like honey to the artist's soul.

Our weekly evaluation meetings can pay tribute to God's faithfulness and our teammates' contributions. If leaders, as well as all participants, permeate these gatherings with a spirit of celebration, those who attend will actually look forward to coming and not dread that our meeting will simply tear down what took place.

Trust

Healthy evaluation meetings develop on a foundation of trust. I wish this commodity could be built overnight, but there really is no shortcut. Over time, teams need to sense deep down that everyone else in the meeting is truly *for them*. The meeting leader must make clear that we gather simply to learn, to give God and the church our very best, and to help one another grow. Defensiveness will diminish in direct proportion to building this kind of supportive environment. Group members will not become vulnerable and speak truth unless they sense that a leader takes seriously the meeting atmosphere. This will most likely require a leader to speak privately with anyone who consistently threatens the trust quotient—and for the leader to model a mature attitude for others to follow. Trust-bashing behaviors often come from these kinds of team members:

- ***Meeting monopolizers*** speak more than anyone else in the group, usually without careful forethought. These chatty individuals are highly opinionated, and their forceful expressions can shut down others. If this is not addressed, the rest of the group begins to resent the constant input, yet may hesitate to disagree or interrupt.

- ***Caustic critics*** have an edge to their critical comments that typically results in hurting the target of their criticism. Caustic comments fill the group with empathy for the person critiqued but make members afraid to be next in line! A leader must privately show the critic a better way to offer critique, or fear will choke the team atmosphere.

- ***Quiet mopers*** say very little verbally, but speak volumes with nonverbal behaviors. Everyone else is uneasy, wondering what these team members really think. A skillful leader seeks to draw out even the most reticent individuals, to bring their thoughts and feelings into the light.

- ***Nervous spiritualizers*** are so concerned that someone might be hurt that they deny truthful words by pointing out, "God can work through our weakness" and "If even one person was reached, we did not labor in vain." Such discounting of truth does not serve a group well. In the end, a leader must guide the team toward accurate, yet loving, evaluation.

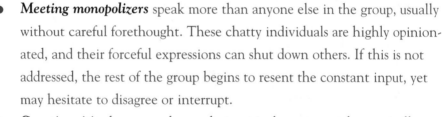

The only way to handle such challenging people is to have the courage to initiate difficult, one-on-one conversations. Years ago, one member of our music staff seemed so fragile in our evaluation meetings that the rest of the group was afraid to tell him anything less than positive. Tom communicated his defensiveness and sensitivity mostly through his eyes, and no one wanted to make those eyes any sadder. Eventually, I knew it was my job to talk privately to this gifted artist. I initiated a meeting and described how his behavior affected the group. To my surprise, Tom was unaware of the signals he was giving off and was sincerely sorry his behavior had made everyone else so uncomfortable. We agreed I would hold him accountable to work on his nonverbal communication and response to constructive criticism. Today, Tom is a champion of receiving feedback, and his growth has encouraged and delighted the group.

Leaders need to lovingly hold up a mirror to any group member whose behavior threatens trust for the delicate evaluation process. Group members, too, can show the mirror to one another and to the leader. Not long ago, two team members asked to meet with me after an evaluation meeting. It was my turn to see how I'd made high-horsepower comments and sweeping statements about a Sunday service—without taking into account the care that had been put into that service. Further, these team members felt I had implied that they'd made incorrect conclusions. Their tone with me was very loving, but, once I saw how my comments had affected them, I knew I needed to apologize. These conversations should always be private, although there are times when an individual's apology to the group can be extremely healing and productive. We have learned to check in with one another after meetings if we even suspect someone might be struggling with what occurred—just a quick phone call or conversation to ask, "Are you okay with what was said?" The healthiest groups are those in which team members can actually speak up in the moment and describe to one another what they are feeling. As each one of us learns to take greater care with our words, the atmosphere of genuine trust will grow stronger.

Carefully Chosen Words

One of the Scripture's hardest commandments for most Christians to follow is "speaking the truth in love" (Ephesians 4:15). It is not a coincidence that the Apostle Paul gives

A printing mistake turned this
24-cent stamp into a collector's item worth $200,000.
The stamp with the upside-down airplane became know as the "Inverted Jenny." This page, however, is not a printing mistake, and is thus worth zilch.

this command in the context of describing true maturity in Christ. Some believers excel at speaking the truth—but lack love. Others are incredibly loving communicators who never have the courage to say hard things. Our senior pastor reminds us frequently that a leader must accept the responsibility to define reality. But how do we define the reality that something did not work well, and yet use words that are constructive rather than hurtful? I tend to dance too delicately around the truth, because I am so afraid I will hurt someone. But pretending that all is well when everyone knows there is trouble in River City serves no one, unless the goal is superficial pleasantness and comfort.

I recall a holiday service that simply missed the mark. We had gathered the congregation to celebrate Thanksgiving Eve and aimed to create a family experience that would move attenders toward genuine praise and thanksgiving to our great God. After the service, a small group of us met in our pastor's office. We were planning to repeat the service two more times, so we gathered to debrief and decide if we needed any changes. As I walked upstairs to that room, I took a deep breath, wondering exactly what I should say. It was not that any element of the service was particularly weak. The problem was we never experienced a deep moment, and the service felt flat.

Clearly our team had put out strong effort, and no one intended the poor result. But my job as a leader was to lovingly, yet truthfully, define reality. So I quickly asked the Holy Spirit for help and expressed what I (and others) had observed. I did not question anyone's work ethic or attitude, but simply described our overall results. We began brainstorming specific ways to make improvements for the next night. I was quick to thank everyone for trying so hard, but made it clear we needed to make changes if we hoped to move the congregation in subsequent services. God helped us adjust the service flow and design comments that would deepen the attenders' experience. It was not a home run, but we certainly got closer to the goal. No one wants to deliver bad news, but sometimes that is precisely what a leader needs to do.

Learning how to communicate constructive criticism is truly an art in itself. Over the years, I have observed individuals who are masters at speaking the truth in love. I have tried to model how champion feedback communicators:

- Acknowledge the subjectivity of evaluating the arts and clearly distinguish among their opinions, trusted others' feedback, and perceived congregational response. (Statements such as "everybody felt. . . " are usually not accurate and therefore not helpful.)
- Do not question the artist's effort—without clear evidence that the person did not give their best.
- Are as specific as possible about what worked and what did not.
- Try to offer specific suggestions for improving the work.
- Avoid highly volatile language and expressions, knowing that words have tremendous power to hurt and are not quickly forgotten.
- Continually come back to the team's mission and target audience.
- Do everything they can to foster a healthy relationship rather than create bitterness and hostility.
- Invite dialog rather than give edicts for change.

People often ask what to do when the senior pastor and arts team disagree about a service element. This is especially tricky if your church does multiple services, and the team meets after the first one to decide whether to repeat, change, or even eliminate an element that didn't work. These exceedingly difficult decisions affect not only the congregation, but also the volunteers who have prepared and sacrificed their time. We recognize that if our arts team and pastor still disagree after genuinely seeking to understand one another's points of view, our pastor has the authority to make the final call. We submit to the senior pastor's leadership and make the change.

I recall one such painful decision after a weekend service where a vocal piece did not, from our pastor's point of view, move people, and did not set up his message in the way we had intended. The arts team hesitated to make a change because, musically, the song had worked well. What made our decision excruciating was that the vocalist and band had performed the song with excellence. The problem was our planning team's poor selection. We had three more weekend services to go, and our pastor requested with great care that we not repeat that song. Our team had to communicate the decision to the vocalist and instrumentalists—speaking the truth in love—and making it absolutely clear that we owned the mistake for choosing the song in the first place. These moments of complete disagreement are extremely rare for us, occurring only a few times a year. But every arts team needs to clarify who has the final say on these issues and then obey Scripture, which admonishes us to "obey your leaders and submit to their authority" (Hebrews 13:17 NIV).

Conducting the Meeting

I will offer guidelines for leading a good evaluation meeting, recognizing that you'll experiment to figure out what works best for your team. First, remember to evaluate the big picture before getting bogged down with details. Just as an individual artist like Rory Noland wants to know first if a song works overall, so a team should discuss how the Sunday service went as a whole, before dissecting its individual parts. The leader can initiate this discussion by asking questions such as:

- Which moments in the service do we believe really touched people? (We base these conversations on team members' own perceptions as well as input they have sought out from others who attended.)
- Should we celebrate any particular parts of the service?
- What atmosphere was created in the room?
- In what ways did people leave church any differently from when they came in?

I recognize that these conversations are always somewhat subjective. We can't measure with absolute accuracy what took place in people's hearts. But discerning team members can, over time, learn to read a room. If a service element was intended to be funny, did the congregation genuinely laugh? If we were aiming to move people, did the response seem authentic, or did it ring false? Encourage team members to show up at the evaluation meeting having

EVALUATION MEETING

already connected with attenders whose perspective they trust, attenders who understand precisely who you are attempting to reach.

After discussing the big picture, you can review your rehearsal process and each element in the service, including transitions. Some arts teams simply talk through the service piece by piece. Others watch all or part of the service on video, starting and stopping to discuss it along the way. It's usually not feasible for every team member to comment on every element, because that takes too long. Sometimes we briefly point out an issue and then set up a separate off-line meeting to untangle details with the appropriate team members.

We ask questions while debriefing each service element. Would we ever choose to repeat that song—why or why not? Was the drama acted out believably—what parts, if any, did not ring true? Do we need to improve on any technical difficulties? How did the arts portion connect with or support the teaching time? What feedback would we want to offer the teaching pastor? Did the service flow in the best order, or would we change it now if we could arrange it differently?

If every evaluation meeting results in two or three key learnings, our time will be well spent. A leader has the difficult role of keeping the meeting from getting too far off track, keeping each individual engaged, and monitoring the balance of celebration and critique. Conducting these meetings requires godly leaders to pray without ceasing for the Holy Spirit's promptings. Above all, a leader must decide how to steer the meeting toward the major learnings that matter most. What can we take away from this meeting that will help us all minister more effectively next week and the week after that? Some teams choose to record their learnings, and others tuck them away in their memory banks to draw from in future brainstorming situations.

The Rewards of Evaluation

As I look back over almost three decades of arts ministry, I am deeply grateful for the legacy of evaluation that began at the back table of a noisy restaurant on early Monday mornings. We have ingrained the value of looking back before we look forward, and without the discipline of feedback, our team would certainly not have grown in excellence and effectiveness. We've learned the hard way to openly admit when we miss the mark and to humbly learn from these mistakes. The best result has been our own personal growth, slowly becoming more humble servants who can actually welcome feedback as a gift. When evaluation becomes a normal way of life for local church ministries, everybody wins, and the kingdom advances step by step, week by week, life by life.

Questions to Explore

1. What is the status of your church's weekly evaluation meetings? Do you schedule consistent meetings at an optimal time?

2. Who are the best people to include in your evaluation meeting? What role, if any, does your pastor have in evaluation? Does the group size and makeup feel right, or should you make adjustments?

3. Assess your own level of defensiveness when you receive loving, constructive feedback. Explore your range of emotions—do you usually experience fear, feel threatened, or stay open to the truth? How defensive are others on your evaluation team?

4. On a scale of 1 to 10, how would you rate the safety of your team's evaluation atmosphere? What would need to change for the number to go up?

5. In the actual flow of the meeting, evaluate whether you generally explore the big picture first or immediately jump to the specific. How often does the team get sidetracked or bogged down by too much detail? What can you do to keep the focus on mission and target audience?

6. Do you feel led to speak privately with any team member about your own behavior in evaluation or about how he or she has acted? With a prayerful, gracious spirit, have the courage to initiate whatever difficult conversations are necessary to create a stronger sense of unity and love on your team as you evaluate together.

chapter **seven**

The
greatest
gift
we can
bring to
ministry
is a
healthy,
joyful,
loving,
vital self.

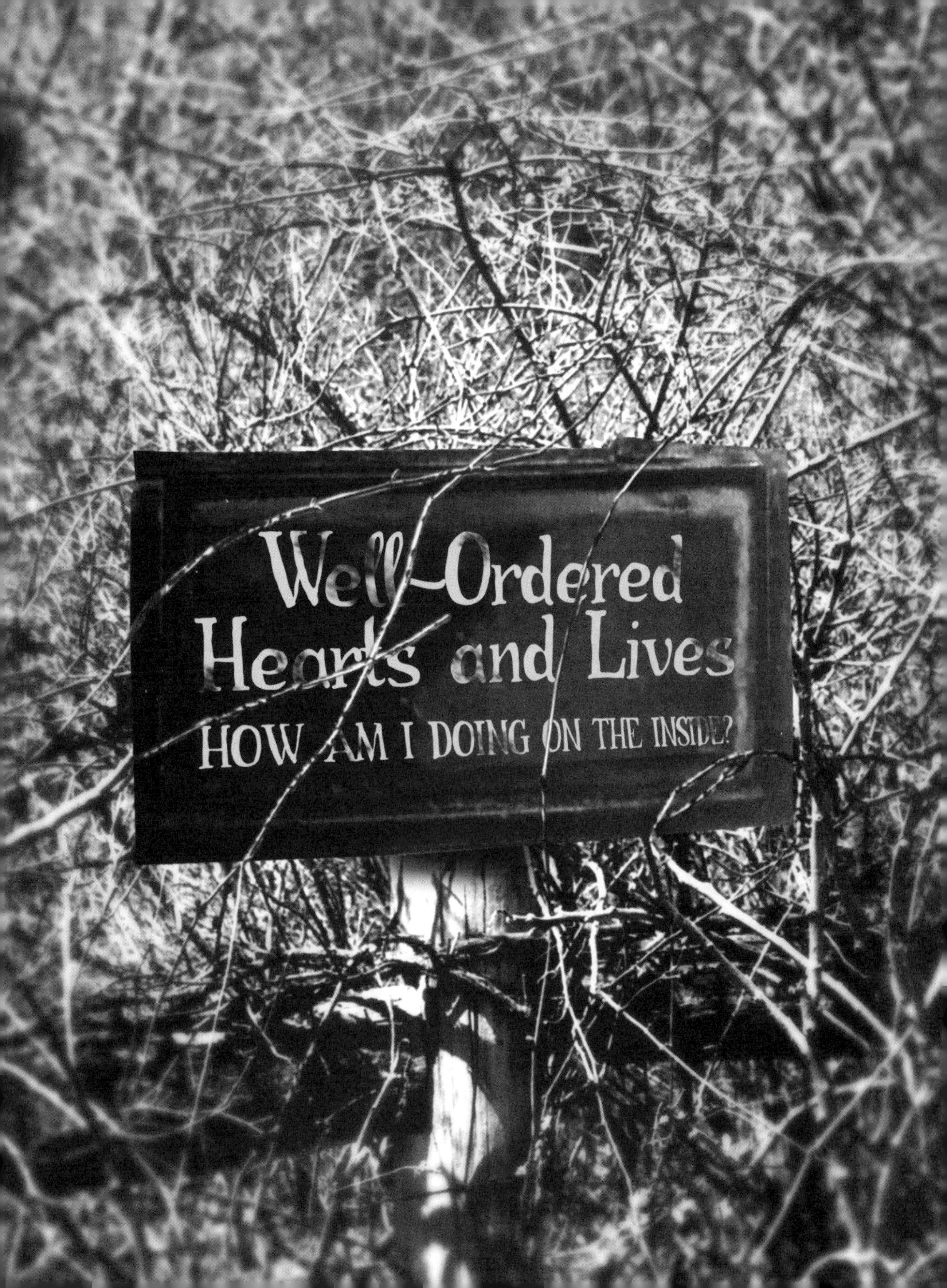
Well-Ordered
Hearts and Lives
HOW AM I DOING ON THE INSIDE?

It was Holy Week—arguably the most significant time of year for Christians and local churches. For over a year our team had been writing a script and music for *Jairus*, an original musical that told the story of our faith in a fresh and compelling way. We designed it as an outreach event so believers could easily invite their unchurched friends. That week the church hummed with excitement. All our serving teams pulled together to support ten performances of this ticketed event. My ten-year-old daughter had a key role in the musical and was having the time of her young life. On opening night I watched from the balcony as thousands of people poured into the auditorium and gazed on the magnificent set. I could see their anticipation grow. Now that all our hard work was about to pay off, I should have been filled with enthusiasm and joy. So why was I sitting there feeling numb, exhausted, and sad? Something inside me was definitely not right.

The process of creating *Jairus* had been destructive for many team members, including me—and my own failings as a leader had contributed to the problem. Our pastor and artists had wrestled over the take-home message of this two-hour experience, and I had failed to bridge the gaps between them with sufficient care, grace, and discernment. We also disagreed about the script, cast selection, and creative decisions during rehearsals. Worse yet, the team was not healthy enough to take on such an enormous challenge. With only minimal adjustments to already overburdened schedules, we simply added the musical on top of everything else we were already doing—regular weekend and mid-week services, multiple conferences, and travel to national and international training events. We limped into it. Despite our difficulties, the end result of the ten performances was positive, even breathtaking. Seeds were sown in our community, and many people considered *Jairus* among our finest work. But the success of the event wasn't enough to make up for what it had cost me. Although I went through the motions of commending our team and faithful volunteers, celebrating what God had apparently done among us, I felt lifeless, without passion, even depressed. In the next weeks and months, I joined my team members in a quest to understand what had gone wrong, to learn from our mistakes and heal my wounded heart and soul.

In staff meetings our senior pastor frequently asks us to remember the greatest gift we can bring to the church. Is it our talents, knowledge, leadership, experience, or creativity? No. These are all important, but not foremost. The greatest gift we can bring to ministry is a healthy, joyful, loving, vital self. *Who we are* as men and women of God matters most. When getting ready for Sundays, my primary job is to get myself ready— to pay close attention to my own heart and soul. The writer of Proverbs states this truth far better than I can, in what would be my life verse—if I had one. The first three words of Proverbs 4:23 boldly declare how essential it is to keep this as our first priority: **"Above all else, guard your heart, for it is the wellspring of life."** Ultimately, we can't bring anything of lasting value to the church or our teams if our own hearts and character are weak, embittered, escapist, or just plain worn out.

Many of us find it exceedingly difficult to do the work we are called to do *and* be the kind of people God asks us to be. If we're not careful, we begin to see ourselves as victims, to make excuses, to look for wiggle room so we can somehow be the exception to rules for godly character. It's not that we don't long to be fully devoted to God, but too often we allow deadline pressures, relentless ministry demands, and overwhelming standards to become excuses for slippage.

In over two decades of ministry, I've seen this unfortunate tendency creep into our artistic team. And I admit the tendency in myself. We don't want to take responsibility—at least not *full* responsibility—for pursuing godliness. It's so much easier to diminish responsibility by making allowances for our perfectionism, artistic personalities, or even our genetic makeup. Or we place the blame elsewhere—an unrealistic schedule, a demanding pastor, out-of-touch elders, difficult team members, a non-supportive spouse—anything or anyone that keeps us from looking in a mirror and facing the hard truth about who we really are behind closed doors.

Okay, if you really want to skip this chapter turn to page 190.

Some may be tempted right now to skip this chapter and move on. I urge you to be courageous and keep reading. We'll explore together six questions we can use to prepare for Sundays. Each question points to a responsibility you and I need to take seriously if we hope to have well-managed hearts, souls, and lives. Use the questions to periodically assess self-management and self-care. In every case, the arrow points directly back at us when we ask the question, "Whose job is it to manage that area?" The right answer will always be *"It's my job!"* As we get ready for Sundays, let's ask ourselves: Am I physically prepared? As far as it depends on me, am I at peace with others? Have I quieted myself before God? Am I showing up with enthusiasm? Is this a week I have to "play hurt"? Am I ready for the unexpected?

Am I Physically Prepared?

Some of us like to believe we can eat a lot of junk food, survive on four or five hours of sleep, avoid exercise, and still—with a quick shot of caffeine—make it all come together on Sunday mornings. In our heads we know there must be a connection between physical health and ministry effectiveness, but far too many artists believe they're exempt. We point to famous writers, musicians, actors, and directors out in the world who consume far too much alcohol or abuse drugs and yet still produce masterful work. How about artists who do their best work at midnight? How can they ever get eight hours sleep? And who has time to exercise regularly with all the pressing demands of ministry, work, and family?

The Bible clearly teaches that you and I are to be responsible stewards of our physical bodies. If we routinely abuse or neglect our physical health, we will pay a price. We won't be able to give God or the church our best contribution over time. In 2 Timothy 2:5, Paul exhorts Timothy, "Follow the Lord's rules for doing his work, just as an athlete either follows the rules or is disqualified and wins no prize" (NLT). Great athletes incorporate daily disciplines into their lives. We all know the big three when it comes to physical health—rest, nutrition, and exercise. So how are we doing in these areas? Do we cave in to the excuse that as artists we are by nature undisciplined and so shouldn't be expected to attend to these things? Do we eat a donut and drink a latte before singing at church or pride ourselves on staying late at a Saturday night party before crawling into Sunday morning rehearsals?

When I think back to the earliest artists at Willow, our physical health was not good. We had a couple of smokers who were trying to quit, we ate too many high-fat foods, and almost no one exercised regularly. I'm thrilled that today most of our team members take these responsibilities quite seriously. But it's an ongoing challenge.

When you look at the big three—rest, nutrition, and exercise—how would you rate yourself on each one? I'm doing well at two out of three. I require at least seven hours of sleep at night. I wish it were not so, but I do. And I function even better on eight! So I've learned I have to go to bed about the same time each night and try to keep a consistent pattern. I'm also disciplined with exercise. When my daughters were little, I aimed to just run three times a week. That was all I could do, and even that felt daunting. But in recent years, I've been able to notch that up to six mornings of exercise a week, with a weight training routine every other day. To be honest, I've been exercising regularly for over twenty-five years, and I'm still waiting to actually like it. I never experience the rush or the high that some people promise. I never wake up in the morning excited to put on my running shoes. I just have to do it. It's a decision I've already made, and I don't give myself permission to miss except on Sundays, or if I'm really sick.

My weakest area is nutrition. (I like to place the blame for this on my Swedish heritage. I see love for pastries and a voracious sweet tooth as part of my DNA.) This is where I most need attention and discipline. I frequently remind myself that all the exercise in the world can't make up for poor eating habits. Of the big three, where do you most shine and where do you perhaps still need work? It is essential to be as healthy as we can be to do our ministry well. Don't we want to be able to serve God and advance the kingdom for as many years as possible? Taking care of physical health plays a huge part in getting ready for Sundays.

Am I at Peace with Others?

Have you ever arrived for church on Sunday morning with a pit in your stomach, knowing there is a barrier between you and another person—a team member, your spouse or child, or even your pastor? This question is based on the Apostle Paul's admonition in Romans 12:18, "If it is possible, as far as it depends on you, live at peace with everyone." It's impossible for us to minister effectively while holding on to anger, hurt, resentment, or envy. No matter how we try to mask and overpower these toxic feelings, they lurk in the shadows and rob us of joy and vitality.

I know this is true for me. And I know it is true for you. When I talk to others in arts ministry, maybe forty percent of our conversation is about strategy, content, and artistic issues. The other sixty percent centers on difficult relationships. Some experience frequent tension with a senior pastor or another team leader. And the hardest part is having the courage to speak the truth in love.

I know what it's like to go through an era when you can't seem to agree with your pastor about what should take place in the services. Bill Hybels and I haven't always walked an easy road together. By their very nature, the arts are somewhat subjective— and both Bill and I have strong viewpoints about what does and doesn't work. To be honest, sometimes we've genuinely wanted to

wait, i think i see a snapping turtle!

WHEN LEADING UP DOESN'T WORK

throw one another in the lake outside our auditorium! On top of that, as our senior pastor, Bill does have authority in the church—if a hard call has to be made, Bill gets to make it. Over the years we have both learned to give and take, to keep short accounts with each other, to speak the truth in love. I dread coming to weekend services if Bill and I are not in a good place with each other. And I accept my responsibility to do whatever I can to be at peace with him and everyone on the team.

I love how Paul's words to Timothy acknowledge that we can't always be at peace with everyone, because sometimes the other person is not willing to reconcile. Paul reminds us that we are to do all *we* can to work out issues, confess when we're wrong, and ask for forgiveness. Before heading into Sundays, we need to be the one willing to *go* to the other person and try to break down the barrier. This holds true for those we live with, those we lead, those we follow, and those who minister at our side. By seeking to live in peace with everyone, we offer our congregations portraits of love and grace. Our message from the platform will transcend the programming and words—it will be a display of unmistakable unity that speaks louder than anything else.

Have I Quieted Myself Before God?

In the film *Saving Private Ryan*, actor Tom Hanks portrays a young military platoon leader. The film begins with the early morning hours of D-Day. Hanks is perched in a gray metal boat, aiming for the beach where he and his platoon will soon land. The camera zooms in on his hands, which shake uncontrollably as he gulps water from his canteen. Two soldiers in front of Hanks throw up—eighteen-year-olds who are smart enough to know they are facing a life-and-death battle and are very much afraid.

When we head into Sunday morning rehearsals and services, it's so easy to lose sight that we, too, are heading into battle. Sundays are truly relentless, arriving every seven days with astonishing predictability. Over time we can forget what is at stake and casually waltz into our church responsibilities. Yet our Enemy, the Evil One, never lets up. He seeks to tear down anything he can, to divide and disrupt and destroy. When we arrive on Sunday morning, it's really game day. This is the time when every rehearsal minute matters, when all our preparations must come together, and, most importantly, when we desperately need God to anoint and empower all that we offer. So many things can go wrong—and so much ministry can go right.

Before we enter the battle, we need intentional quiet and solitude, times in which we connect with our Commander-in-Chief. In all the days leading up to Sunday, and even on our drive to church, we must pause to prepare our souls. I'm not suggesting we become so anxious we all lose our breakfasts like fear-stricken soldiers or walk into church with uncontrollably shaking hands. But deep down, we can cultivate a sober mind and heart about what's at stake. We can acknowledge our acute need to abide in the only One able to bear fruit that will remain.

For a recent weekend message called "God Is Our Refuge," we prepared a service to provide hope for those experiencing pain or loss. During my short drive to church, I fought off the desire to zone out. I didn't tune in to hear the deep voice of a favorite radio personality talk about the Chicago arts scene. Instead, I spent a few moments in silence, remembering specific people in our community who desperately needed God's comfort. One family had just lost their forty-seven-year-old husband and father. I knew they planned to drag themselves to church that day, so I offered up a prayer for them and others like them. In those brief moments I was reminded again of what is at stake in the hour on Sunday. As I walked into church, my heart was ready to do my part.

Whenever you and I get too busy to spend time in solitude with our Savior, we are simply too busy. It's our job to culti-vate healthy souls by pruning what needs to be cut away.

No matter how much I want to think the job of spiritual nurture belongs to my pastor, the elders, my husband, or small group friends, the truth is that only I can be held responsible. I urge you to head into Sunday morning battles centered and healthy, so God can pour his power through you.

Am I Showing Up with Enthusiasm?

Gordy and his wife, Barb, serve on our production crew. Their children are grown, and for now this couple has chosen to invest in building community on our backstage team, helping to set up stage equipment and props and diligently praying for everything that takes place in our services. Gordy is a big man with twinkling eyes and a balding head. Like the rest of our crew, he always wears black clothing so he can fade into the background while setting up props on stage during a service.

When I arrive, Gordy has been working for a couple hours. He always greets me with a warm smile and inquires, "How can I specifically pray for you? Is there anything in this service that most concerns you?" Often my response fills Gordy's eyes with tears. During rehearsals, Gordy provides an enthusiastic audience for actors and musicians who wonder if their material will connect. He laughs the loudest and is the first one to let them know if he's been deeply moved. Before the service begins, Gordy leads a circle of crewmembers in passionate prayer for God to work mightily among and through us. Between services, Gordy is the master of encouragement, letting all of us know that the part we played truly mattered.

I've been reflecting on how this one volunteer affects me every time I show up to serve at church. What if Gordy always appeared listless, unengaged, or even slightly sarcastic? What if he simply went through the motions, doing his menial tasks without enthusiasm? The rest of us would be the losers. Gordy lifts us to a higher level; he ennobles us.

Every person contributing to the hour on Sunday—no matter what their role— affects the rest of the team by their attitude. Just a look of disgust or disdain can quench someone's spirit. But when one of us shows up with a joyful spirit, feeling it's a privilege to serve and seeking out others we can encourage, we profoundly influence team culture. I long to be more like Gordy. It's my responsibility, regardless of whatever is going on in my life, to arrive at church with positive energy, knowing that my attitude rubs off on others.

Is this a Week I Have to "Play Hurt"?

Chicagoans hold tightly to memories of a bygone era when our Chicago Bulls dominated the NBA. The Bulls have been so pathetic in recent years that we continually rewind our thoughts to the Michael Jordan era, when it seemed like they could never lose. No Bulls fan can forget the fifth game of a playoff series against the Utah Jazz. The night before the game, Jordan came down with either altitude sickness or food poisoning—no one was ever sure. Biographer David Halberstam writes that the team trainer "rushed to Jordan's room and found him curled up in a fetal position, wrapped in blankets and pathetically weak. He had not slept at all. He had an intense headache and had suffered violent nausea throughout the night. The greatest player in the world looked like a frail, weak zombie. It was inconceivable that he might play that day."

Though frail and haggard, Jordan was determined to play. Because of his efforts, the Bulls were down only four points at the half. He limped into the locker room at halftime appearing uncharacteristically pale and listless. He looked horrible. "But what he looked like and what he was doing on the floor when it mattered were two separate things," continued Halberstam. Jordan came back and won the game with a three-point shot, having scored 38 points overall. Halberstam summed it up: "It had been an indelible performance, an astonishing display of spiritual determination; he had done nothing less than give a clinic in what set him apart from everyone else in his profession."

You and I won't always be at 100-percent vitality heading into Sundays. There are weeks we won't feel great physically. There are even more weeks when we'll struggle emotionally or spiritually. And yet we must dig down deep and minister with whatever strength God provides. That's what playing hurt means. It's showing up on Sunday with a lump in our throats, saying, "God, I don't feel very useful today. I'm wounded and weary. But I'll give you whatever I've got and ask you to somehow bear fruit through my weakness." Sometimes soldiers have to go into battle when they're not

God, how am i Supposed to lead worship with this thing in my mouth?

at their best. That's often when God does his most astonishing work.

Okay, don't panic! the service starts in ten minutes and preacher bob wants to change the message from SPIRITUALITY to SEXUALITY.

Am I Ready for the Unexpected?

The answer to the final question is one I keep learning and re-learning. Am I ready for the unexpected on Sunday mornings? Whatever your role is on Sundays, I'm sure that, like me, you come in with a plan. But quite often, things do not go according to plan. A volunteer is sick or late. A microphone, monitor, light, or some other equipment simply doesn't work. Rehearsing a drama sketch or worship music requires ten more minutes than we allocated. An electrical storm blows out our power. The pastor comes in to tell us God has led him to rewrite his last two sermon points, and our programming elements no longer fit the teaching!

Rather than being surprised by the unexpected, I am learning to expect it. It's part of the deal. We can either choose to panic and lose all self-control *or* we can see each surprise as an opportunity for ministry and try to discern how God would have us respond. The unexpected also includes what takes place surrounding service times.

For several years we had four weekend services—two on Saturday night and two on Sunday morning. Giving a message at four back-to-back services drained me. One weekend when I was teaching, I headed between Sunday morning services to the area we call "the tunnel," where our volunteers gather. I planned to get a cup of tea and head to my office to collect myself before teaching again. But God had a different plan.

A veteran production volunteer was sitting at a table in the tunnel, her eyes filled with tears. No one else was sitting near her. I wanted so badly to keep walking, hoping God would send someone to meet her need. I had been pouring myself out all weekend and thought I deserved a break. But the Holy Spirit prompted me to stop and ask this young woman what was going on. She blurted out her story about a difficult situation at work and a hard decision she was facing. I listened and then fed back to her what she already knew was right to do. I asked if I could pray with her. The entire encounter took only fifteen minutes. As I walked back to my office, I thought about how ministry in that moment for one person was every bit as significant in God's eyes as what I do up front for thousands. Every moment on Sundays matters, even those brief times in the cracks, when we look in a person's eyes and seek to reflect Christ's unconditional love.

We all need to hold our well-laid plans somewhat loosely as we head into Sundays. For those of us who are control freaks, this is really hard! But God sees the whole scene more comprehensively than we ever can. He asks us to listen to his whispers at each point along the way and trust him to guide us. It's truly our job to arrive on Sundays ready for the unexpected.

An Artist's Version of 1 Corinthians 13

I so easily forget that no matter how powerful our Sunday services may be, no matter how much fruit God bears, it will all evaporate if I do not serve with love. One day I decided to write my own version of the first few verses of 1 Corinthians 13 (sometimes referred to as the "love chapter") to redirect my focus from ministry activity toward managing my heart:

If I communicate the most incredibly passionate and eloquent moment for our congregation, but have not love, I am only a resounding gong or a clanging cymbal. If I build effective volunteer teams and creatively unleash the arts for the hour on Sunday, but have not love, I am nothing. If I serve the longest hours and earn acclaim for my leadership of artists, but have not ♥, I gain nothing.

Create your own Artist's Version of 1 Corinthians 13 or photocopy this page and cut along the dotted lines. Hang it where you will see it everyday.

And then I return to the Apostle Paul's description of love:

Love is patient, love is kind. It does not envy, it does not boast, it is not proud. It does not dishonor others, it is not self-seeking, it is not easily angered, it keeps no record of wrongs. Love does not delight in evil but rejoices with the truth. It always protects, always trusts, always hopes, always perseveres. Love never fails.

I could read those words every day of my life—and still I would fall short. When all is said and done, I long for my life's work to first and foremost be about love. I cannot just wish it to be so—I must zealously guard my heart, alert to forces that seek everyday to deaden and distract me. Ezekiel 36:26 reminds me that God is in the heart-transforming business: "I will give you a new heart and put a new spirit in you; I will remove from you your heart of stone and give you a heart of flesh." As I cooperate with God's gracious work on my heart, I will give to him, my family, my team, and my church the greatest gift I can possibly give. I urge you to accept your responsibility for a well-managed heart and life.

Questions to Explore

1. Of the big three for physical health (rest, exercise, and nutrition), which area or areas are strong for you? Where do you need the most improvement?

2. Can you think of anyone you must reconcile with, so you can say that "as far as it depends on you," you are at peace with others? What would be your next step toward peace?

3. Evaluate how consistently you allow time for solitude and other spiritual disciplines within the rhythm of your week. Is there anything you need to work on to enter Sundays with a more centered heart?

4. Think of a team member who shows up for rehearsals and services with enthusiasm. Resolve to express gratitude to that individual. How would you rate your own attitude coming into Sundays?

5. Have you ever had to "play hurt" on a Sunday? Recall what that felt like and how equipped you were to minister out of weakness.

6. Remember a recent time when the unexpected took place on Sunday morning at your church. How did you and others respond?

7. Of the six major issues (represented by the questions to ask when heading into Sundays), which do you commit to improve on in the coming weeks? What will be your first steps?

part two

Riding Home
from Sundays

I've secretly wished the cars of all
church attenders could be fitted with
a secret listening device so we could
hear people's comments about the
service as they drive home from
church! The core values in this
section are all about what we long
for people to experience in the hour
on Sunday, and each is described in
terms of statements we'd love to
hear people say on the ride home
after the service.

chapter **eight**

I sometimes
allow myself
to dream
about what
would
happen if
the church
once again
became
known as
the place
where
outstanding
art was
created
for God.

Excellence
"THAT WAS GOOD!"

THE ♥value of excellence

Several years ago our team had the privilege of leading a three-day conference for church leaders in Auckland, New Zealand—one of the most beautiful cities we've ever visited. We drank in the sunny weather and the outrageously generous hospitality of the natives, affectionately known as *Kiwis*. We also worked hard. Mastering unfamiliar technical equipment and preparing powerful drama, music, and video segments required early morning rehearsals and long days. By the middle of the second day, we began to hear mutterings from some attenders who questioned our commitment to excellence. Their basic message was, "Why don't you relax? This is just a church event." On the third day, the issue came up in a question-and-answer session with our senior pastor. I'll never forget Bill's response.

Bill described a lunchtime walk he'd taken that day near Auckland's harbor. A devoted sailor, Bill closely observed renowned New Zealand racing teams zealously practicing their starts for an upcoming America's Cup race. He explained how the racers scrambled to shave mere seconds off their start times, knowing that the regatta's start often determines the winner. Shouting instructions to one another for improved performance, crewmembers relentlessly perfected their craft.

Then came the punch line. Bill looked at our good-natured New Zealand friends and said, "You can't convince me that the value of excellence doesn't exist in your culture. Without it you wouldn't be known as the finest sailors in the world. Why don't we bring that same devotion to church work, where the stakes are infinitely higher—because human lives can be transformed for all eternity? Should we not apply this God-given capacity for excellence to the most significant endeavor on the planet, which is building vital local churches?" The room grew uncomfortably quiet.

The tension and mixed feelings about excellence are not unique to Kiwis—I surely don't want to pick on them! We've encountered similar protests across Europe, South Africa, Canada, and throughout the United States. No other value described in this book causes more controversy and confusion.

When it comes to excellence, my strongest desire is that people would drive home from church declaring, "That was good!" But what lies behind this desire? Is it pride rooted in a childish need for approval? Is it a competitive drive to be the best no matter what the cost? Or is excellence a legitimate and God-honoring value worthy of pursuit? Somewhere along the way, many of us have been misguided in our understanding of the excellence value.

Excellence Wrongly Understood

For most of us, the word *excellence* evokes an assortment of personal experiences, many of them negative. We may remember a schoolteacher who told our parents we weren't working up to our potential. Perhaps we were forced to practice musical scales over and over until we wanted to scream. Or maybe there was a difficult boss whom we could never please no matter how hard we tried. These misunderstandings of true excellence often cause us to default to one of two extremes—mediocrity or perfectionism—both of which dishonor God.

Mediocrity

No phrase uttered by Christian leaders stirs my wrath more than this one: "It's only church." The unstated assumptions are that what happens in the hour on Sunday isn't important enough to warrant passionate energy and effort, that neither the attenders nor God expect all that much of us, and that we should all just chill out. While few of us want to admit to these thoughts, they lurk in the shadows and directly impact how we do ministry. Such views are usually rooted in fear or laziness.

Fear is often the underlying reason for mediocrity. **Fear of failure immobilizes countless artists and teachers.** We fear disappointing the pastor, the team, or the congregation. Most of all, we are afraid of failing ourselves. If we aim for a high standard, how will we handle it if we can't achieve the goal? I had to deal with fear of failure as I prepared to write this book. I deeply respect quality writing and love great literature. A few years ago when someone suggested I write a book, I hesitated, largely because I knew I'd never be able to craft prose as well as my favorite authors—Frederick Buechner, Anne Lamott, and Pat Conroy. Every time I write a sentence, I read it back, hoping it will magically sound like the writing of one of my heroes. It

never does! Many of us reason that if we can't do a job without risking failure, it's better not to try so hard—to choose mediocrity—so we can live with ourselves.

There are a host of other fears related to excellence in church services. Some fear that pursuing excellence puts an excessive emphasis on production values. None of us wants words and phrases like **SLICK** **outrageou$ly expen$ive** *over-the-top*

or *massively complicated* to describe the hour on Sunday. We are also afraid that focusing on excellence might result in neurotic, unhealthy team behaviors and an unbalanced emphasis on human effort over the Holy Spirit's more important work. We don't want to be accused of competing with other churches, trying to woo attenders with a "better show" or keep from losing them to a church with a bigger choir or flashier technology.

Most of all, we desperately want to avoid caving into the world's obsession with superstars, ratings, and the latest, greatest techniques. Church should be distinguished from all that insanity, we reason. And so we slide toward mediocrity, because we are afraid and don't know what to do with all these understandable concerns.

Others live in the extreme of mediocrity not because they are afraid but, truth be told, because they simply don't want to work all that hard. We can even spiritualize our lack of quality by saying God will do his mighty work no matter what, and we don't want to take any earthly credit! I know of music directors who select songs at the very last minute, throwing a service order together with almost no rehearsal or forethought, in the casual trust that somehow the Spirit will anoint it anyway.

Some church leaders justify mediocrity in a misguided effort to protect their volunteers. They resist asking volunteers to sacrifice time for rehearsal or early Sunday morning preparation on the grounds that they just can't demand so much of their people. In many cases, these leaders choose not to work hard themselves, and they would be surprised to discover most volunteers prefer to invest additional time so they can feel more adequately prepared. When we fail to diligently craft the hour on Sunday, I wonder how God feels about our desperate prayers, launched two minutes before the service, begging him to show up and transform the congregation's hearts.

Perfectionism

Excellence's opposite extreme is perfectionism—an unhealthy obsession that robs joy and slays spirits. In my early years as a Christian artist and leader, I struggled mightily with perfectionism. Sunday afternoons were often the most painful time of my week. My husband would glance at my sour face as he attempted to watch a football game and inquire, "What's the matter?" I would proceed to tell him every little thing that had gone wrong in that morning's service. Most of my observations had eluded Warren, an average, non-artistic attender. Like the coach of a losing team, I replayed and agonized over every moment—the off-tempo song, an actor's missed line—that hadn't lived up to my original vision. My distorted perspective made it difficult to rejoice that the service may have changed lives. What a sick woman!

My guess is I'm not alone in my journey to recover from perfectionism. This neurotic tendency plagues countless Christian artists, leaders, and teachers. Our pursuit of perfection often leads to excessive work hours, as we reason that with just a little more time, we can reach our standard. Many of us end up way out of balance, devoting too little time to family, fun, and friendship. None of us can be healed overnight. We need to engage in a constant reprogramming of the voices that scream lies to us, lies proclaiming that nothing less than perfect is acceptable, that we are total failures. My wake-up call to my serious perfectionism came almost twenty years ago, on the night of a major church outreach event.

For the first time under my leadership, our artists had crafted an original two-hour experience of music, drama, and dance to introduce basic Christianity to our lost friends. My role as producer included calling key technical cues from the production booth. I missed a couple of the cues. They weren't really total misses; my timing just wasn't as perfect as I'd hoped. But everything else, as I later discerned, had gone beautifully. Nevertheless, I was angry with myself for not doing what I deemed a perfect job. I avoided team members, not giving them the encouragement they richly deserved. I rushed to my car that night, fighting back tears. I cried most of the way home. Once again, my husband—Joe Average attender—hadn't noticed any mistakes at all.

The next morning our music director, Rory Noland, called me to check in. He commended me on producing a wonderful event and asked why I had vanished the night before. With a quivering voice, I told Rory of my deep disappointment and apologized for "ruining" the night when everyone else had done such a stellar job. Rory was shocked. He tried to convince me that my perceptions were way off and that my mistakes hadn't affected the results at all. I thanked him but secretly concluded he was only trying to make me feel better.

When I arrived at the office the next day, a small painting in a wooden frame sat on my desk. It was a lovely splash of pastel watercolors. I also noticed a small black ink dot in the lower right corner. Next to the frame was a card from Rory, which read:

> Our son Micah painted this watercolor of a sunset yesterday. Isn't it a good painting? Unfortunately, just as we were ready to frame it, a small ink dot accidentally spilled on the canvas. But it's still a beautiful sunset, don't you agree?

In that moment I saw the truth. I was looking only at the dots. Whenever we created services or events, it was the mistakes I seized on and could never let go of. I was obsessed with our dots. As a result, my own spirit and the team's morale suffered. Even though I tried to hide it, they could sense my severe disappointment. I robbed the team and myself of the freedom that comes from knowing God can work through our best efforts even when they aren't perfect. Fruit can be borne and lives transformed despite human failings and shortcomings. Rory's creative dot story prompted me to face my perfectionism and to seek healing from its dangerous clutches. Our team began to refer to perfectionism as the

DOT SYNDROME

and challenged one another to not cave into that temptation. Years later, I can see how God has graciously cooperated with my efforts to root out this misguided understanding of excellence. I'm not all the way there, but I can now look beyond the dots and focus on the beauty of the bigger picture. And my husband enjoys being with me on Sunday afternoons again!

Excellence Rightly Understood

If we hope to move away from mediocrity or perfectionism toward a better understanding of excellence, it's helpful to remember that most magnificent art originated in the church—the finest music, paintings, sculpture, and writing. In his wonderful book *Imagine*, writer Steve Turner describes the period when the church of Rome was at the center of European power:

> [The church] was the major sponsor of painting and sculpture. Michelangelo's best-known work was commissioned directly by various popes, and he was eventually made chief architect of St. Peter's, Rome. Raphael did work for individual churches and cathedrals. Much of Bosch's art was paid for by the Brotherhood of Our Lady, a Christian fraternity of which he was a member.

Church buildings were also beautiful. Whether ornate cathedrals or simple gathering places, these structures were crafted of the finest materials by the world's most skilled artisans. The very idea that the arts in church could be anything less than excellent would have been unthinkable to believers in former centuries. So how did we lose our way?

I am not a history expert, and I would be the last to place specific blame. I only know that in the latter part of the twentieth century and now in the twenty-first, churches are no longer known as standard bearers for excellence in architecture or the arts. Over twenty years ago I read *Addicted to Mediocrity*, a little book by Franky Schaeffer that helped me make sense of the decline of quality among Christian artists. Mr. Schaeffer boldly stated what I intuitively knew to be true: "The modern Christian world and what is known as evangelicalism in general is marked, in the area of the arts and cultural endeavor, by one outstanding feature, and that is its *addiction to mediocrity*." That last phrase served as more than just a provocative title for the book—it was a clarion call for revolution. It was time for artists in the church to reclaim their God-given gifts and devote themselves to excellence. Schaeffer's words inspire me to this day:

Of all people, Christians should be addicted to quality and integrity in every area, not looking for excuses for second-best. We must resist this onslaught. We must demand higher standards. We must look for people with real creative integrity and talent, or we must not dabble in these creative fields at all. All of this does not mean that there is no room for the first halting steps, for experimentation, for mistakes and for development. But it does mean that there is no room for lazy, entrenched, year-after-year established mediocrity, unchanging and unvaried.

At about the same time I was reading Franky Schaeffer's book, my pastor was wrestling with his understanding of excellence.

who is Malachi?

i don't know.
i think an Italian prophet.

A Lesson from Malachi

Bill was reading Malachi 1, an Old Testament passage that left an indelible mark on his thinking and, ultimately, on our church. In this passage, the Lord Almighty responds with disgust and outright anger to his people's second-rate sacrifices. Instead of bringing God their prime animals to place on the altar, the Israelites were scouring their flocks for injured, crippled, and diseased animals. God calls their half-hearted, lazy displays of worship "contemptible." He boldly declares that his people have profaned the Lord's Table and he refuses to accept their pathetic attempts to please him. God saw right through their mediocrity.

Through this story, the Holy Spirit impressed upon Bill that we must offer God our very best—our prime sacrifices—in every aspect of ministry and building the church. As Bill teaches our congregation, *"Excellence honors God and inspires people."* Our church is indebted to our pastor for calling us to the highest possible standard in every area of ministry—from how we take care of our buildings and property to how we teach children, serve the poor, create effective student and adult ministries, and on and on. Everyone at the core of our church considers it unacceptable to give any less than 100 percent. Another of Bill's teachings is that 95 percent devotion is 5 percent short! Our members can't leave a church bathroom looking unkempt. We pick up litter from our lawns and plant beautiful flowers every spring to reflect our Creator's majesty. Even in our formative years in the rented movie theater, we spent early morning hours cleaning up popcorn and mopping sticky floors so we could invite folks into as immaculate a "sanctuary" as possible. Our church is far from perfect, but we do our absolute best to make it excellent.

$$\begin{array}{r} 100\% \\ = \; 95\% \\ \hline \text{Five \%} \end{array}$$

100 percent
95 PERCENT
5% short

The value of excellence first permeates the hearts of individuals. As they model it for others, it isn't long before excellence becomes a way of life in the church. People joyfully show up expecting to serve with their sleeves rolled up, their minds fully engaged, and their radars on high alert to discern potential improvements. We've learned that devotion to excellence really does inspire our visitors. They come to church for the first time expecting it to be second-rate and thrown together. When they experience the opposite, they are both surprised and motivated to investigate the faith behind the quality.

A New Definition

If excellence is not about mediocrity or perfectionism, what is it about? Webster's dictionary describes excellence as "surpassing goodness" and something that is excellent as "outstandingly good of its kind." Awhile back, a friend offered a definition that gives us a different, more helpful handle. He said that excellence is *doing the best you can with what you have*. What a freeing idea! This definition moves me from perfectionism to giving my all, from any sense of competition to an honest assessment of my resources. What is excellent for one person or church may only be mediocre for another. Our sole responsibility is to steward what we have with our absolute best effort. Colossians 3:23 (NLT) puts it this way: "Work hard and cheerfully at whatever you do, as though you were working for the Lord, rather than for people." We serve a God who has only ever given us his absolute best. In return he asks for nothing less from us.

The church planters who recently launched Discovery Church in Voorhees, New Jersey, inspire me toward excellence. Pastor Randy Smith and his small band of adventurers envisioned, planned, and prayed for several months before their first hour on Sunday. Because their services are held in a middle school gym, this dedicated team designed what they call "church in a box." They built systems they could roll in, plug in, and use for sound, media, children's ministry, ushers, bookstore, and café. They store everything in large rolling boxes that are completely self-contained, clearly labeled, and hauled out of an old white cube truck. With a tiny

Unload
Discove
Church

doing the best with what have ^ we

Discovery Church
Bookstore!

team of volunteers, Discovery Church is set up and ready to rehearse in just forty-five minutes! Pastor Randy is appropriately proud when he describes his faithful team as those who are "committed to doing it right." This brand new community of faith is already seeing results—God is anointing their efforts and people far from God are coming to faith. The Discovery team is doing the best they can with what they have.

Practicing Excellence

Before we move on to how we can practice the value of excellence, it's important to honestly assess our ministries and ourselves. Are we more inclined toward a lazy acceptance of mediocrity or toward an obsessive pursuit of perfectionism? As Christian artists and leaders pursue godliness and emotional health, we will increasingly move toward the middle and away from either extreme. On the continuum below, where would you place an X to describe your own tendencies?

Mediocrity   Perfectionism

We need to devote ourselves, without apology, to giving God and the church our absolute best. This devotion to excellence will cost us. It does not come easily or cheaply. All who uphold this value will pay a price when we choose to raise aesthetic standards, develop gifts, invest in rehearsal time, and allocate money to support the arts.

Raise Aesthetic Standards

A few years back on vacation in upstate New York, I purchased a last-minute ticket to a concert featuring the outstanding cellist Yo-Yo Ma. As I sat among strangers in an outdoor pavilion under magnificent starlight on that sticky summer night, this passionate man and his beloved instrument created transfixing music. Its beauty made my heart ache with joy. I have had similar moments of awe while encountering Julie Taymor's dazzling set and costume designs in *The Lion King*; Tom Stoppard's magnificent writing in his Broadway play *Arcadia*; Rembrandt's masterful paintings at Chicago's Art Institute; Susan Stroman's stunning choreography in *The Producers*. Witnessing an artist's greatness deepens our appreciation of what is really good and elevates our standards of excellence and beauty.

Go out of your way to read excellent literature, attend the best concerts and theater you can afford, wander in art museums, and listen to the finest recordings in a variety of musical genres. All this input enriches our minds and hearts with possibilities, with a picture of extraordinary art at its best. And in ways we can't always measure, we will become pursuers of excellence.

Develop Gifts

It is our responsibility to steward and develop whatever gifts our Creator has given us. This is a life-long devotion to getting better at whatever we bring to the body of Christ. And everyone—no matter how gifted—can always improve. This is true of musicians, teachers, actors, writers, painters, sound engineers, lighting designers, and every other team member. As the Apostle Paul advised his disciple Timothy

OR SEE GREAT STUFF!

uh guys? i think i have an idea.

concerning teaching gifts: "Do not neglect your gift. . . Be diligent in these matters; give yourself wholly to them, so that everyone may see your progress" (1 Timothy 4:14–15).

I believe that serious development of our gifts should be considered a normal part of church culture. As I walk through our staff offices, I frequently hear an instrumentalist practicing or a vocalist taking a weekly lesson to develop his or her craft. It's inspiring to know these individuals are stretching themselves, repeating a piece of music over and over again to improve. On Tuesday evenings our volunteer drama team usually trains in improvisation or rehearses scenes from plays. Although it's unlikely they'll ever perform these improvisations and scenes in a church service, creating new characters equips our actors in significant ways. Our technical team leaders look for workshops to help their teams stay current with the latest developments in lighting, sound, and video. They also subscribe to professional journals to keep abreast of new advances in their fields. Christ-followers must be as serious about stewarding and nurturing their gifts as they are about growing as disciples.

Many artists and teachers develop their gifts by learning from a mentor—someone who is farther along and can provide coaching and perspective. Constructive feedback from a person who has observed your gift in action will help you see where you are strong and where you still need improvement. The best mentors and coaches provide specific, frequent feedback, as well as strong doses of encouragement. For many years, Corinne Ferguson—currently our weekend services director—served as a vocal coach for our team's volunteer vocalists. In the private sanctuary of her inviting office, Corinne provided a safe place for these vocalists to observe a video of their last ministry opportunity. She celebrated with them what they did well, gently offered suggestions for next steps, and then provided an opportunity for the vocalist to experiment with new techniques for an audience of one (Corinne). I often teased Corinne that she was actually part vocal coach and part therapist. Her one-hour sessions typically included dialog about the student's life struggles as

corinne
at work

well as the vulnerability of singing in front of many people and seeking to communicate authentically. The vocalists' progress demonstrates the results of Corinne's mentoring. I long for every Christian artist to receive the priceless gift of such a coach.

Invest in Rehearsal Time

A professional golfer once said, "The more I practice, the luckier I get." That quip reminds us that excellence is not about magic—it is the result of hard work and long hours of preparation. I often overhear attenders ponder the quality of our arts ministry for services or conferences, as if it can be traced only to some amazing miracle. I trace the wonder of transformed lives to the miraculous, supernatural work of God, but the quality of the arts themselves is the result of artists who are willing to invest the time required to be confident and strong. In many ways, the so-called secret to excellence is actually the mundane, relentless process of living with the material and rehearsing it until it seems to come naturally. The reality of doing the work is not sexy—it's actually somewhat tedious. It requires coming out on cold winter nights to rehearse in small rooms until the music, script, or dance is grounded and sure. It requires vocalists who warm-up in early morning hours, dancers who faithfully stretch their muscles, and percussionists who bang on drums in their basements. It requires a team of technicians who carefully maintain equipment, who aim lights until they are just right, who are given enough time to practice with the artists so they, too, can do their job well.

People often ask, "How do you get your volunteers to do all this work?" Many church leaders are hesitant to set high standards for their teams. They feel apologetic about asking for even brief rehearsal times. I have learned that almost all volunteers respond to leaders who call out the very best in them. Deep down, volunteers really want to give God their devoted efforts, and they don't want to be embarrassed by poor efforts on the stage. When they consistently see the results of their investments in rehearsal time, when they feel confident and prepared to serve, and most of all, when they experience the wonder of being used by God to help transform lives—then they are more than willing to pay the price for excellence. In fact, they often ask if we can rehearse a little longer! Volunteers don't want to feel rushed, tentative, or tense as they head into services. We need to provide them with adequate preparation, along with time to pray together, so they can enter the hour on Sunday with a sense of peace and anticipation of all God might do.

Show Me the Money

Earlier in this chapter, I stated that excellence doesn't have to be expensive. It is true that even the simplest parts of a service can be done with quality. But I would be less than honest if I didn't admit there is a financial cost to developing excellent church services week after week. A thriving arts ministry doesn't come for free. It costs money to secure staff, equipment, and materials to create memorable moments and church-wide events.

When we began Willow Creek in a rented movie theater, we literally had no money. A small team of young people sold tomatoes door-to-door—I'm not kidding!—to raise enough money to pay the rent and purchase basic sound and lighting equipment. For the first year, all our resources went to programming services before any staff received salaries. We knew we had to place a disproportionate emphasis on our weekend services just to get this church off the ground. Throughout our history, as scores of other ministries have developed and needed funding, we have continued to allocate enough money to do a quality job on Sunday morning. This doesn't mean we have all the latest and greatest technical equipment. Our team certainly doesn't get everything we long for and request. But our board and elders understand that if we want powerful music, drama, dance, and video supported by quality sound and lighting, we have to allocate adequate funds. Unfortunately, the price tag on capital equipment for the arts is far more expensive than the average person would ever guess. It's vitally important that arts ministry teams prioritize what is most needed and gradually add equipment and staff as funds are provided. We must periodically let church leaders know the barriers we face to taking the next step in our ministry and ask for their ongoing support.

No Regrets

I sometimes allow myself to dream about what would happen if the church once again became known as the place where outstanding art was created for God. Imagine if even people far from our Creator visited churches expecting quality, power, and effective communication of truth. Could we ever restore such a positive reputation? A transformation of public opinion requires steady change—church by church, year by year, Sunday by Sunday. As we simply strive to get a little better each week, to inspire and equip our volunteers, over time this dream really could come true. God would be glorified and lives would be changed.

Scripture describes a day when each one of us will individually face our Lord and account for what we did with what was entrusted to us. On that day, I don't want to sheepishly apologize for failing to develop my own gifts, for shirking careful preparation for ministry, for giving God's church any less than I was able to give. Just as I long for attenders to leave church remarking, "That was good!" I hope my heavenly Father will say those words to me.

"Nancy, you were not perfect, and every time you used your gift was not a home run. But bottom line... well done. That was good."

My friends, let's not be too afraid or too lazy to strive for excellence. I believe all of us long to hear our Creator say,

'Well done."

We can do the best we can with what we have. That is all he asks.

Questions to Explore

1. Where would you place yourself and your team on the continuum between mediocrity and perfectionism?

2. If you admit to being more inclined toward mediocrity, identify what fears might underlie that tendency—fear of failure, fear of the perception of "slickness," fear of appearing competitive, or fear of not relying on the Holy Spirit. Or is your mediocrity based in an avoidance of working too hard yourself or asking for more from volunteers? Dig deep to diagnose your leanings toward mediocrity and bring them out into the light.

3. If you admit to struggling more with perfectionism, recall a recent time when you "saw only the dots" in a service and could not celebrate what God had done as a result. What steps can you take toward a healthier perspective?

4. Using the definition that excellence is doing the best you can with what you have, evaluate your own current level of pursuing excellence as well as the level of excellence at your church. In what areas can you take specific steps to improve?

5. What is the last experience of great art you exposed yourself to? What is next on your list?

6. Are you intentionally developing your gifts? If not, what is required to make this a reality? Have you ever been developed by a mentor in your gift area? If so, describe how that experience contributed to your growth.

7. Explore whether your team devotes adequate rehearsal time for preparing the hour on Sunday. If not, what adjustments could you make to help every artist (including the technical teams) feel more confident and prepared?

chapter nine

I
will
never
get
over
the
power
of a
great
idea.

The day was supposed to be all about baseball. As a Valentine's Day gift, I promised my husband a visit to the Field Museum of Natural History in Chicago, where famous artifacts of our national pastime were assembled in a traveling exhibit called *Baseball As America*. I looked forward to seeing his boyish delight as he immersed himself in displays about his childhood heroes and relived magic moments at Wrigley Field and Yankee Stadium. (The baseball cards he collected as a boy would now be worth a small fortune—if his well-meaning mother had not tossed them in the garbage can.) At the elegant museum's ticket counter, we discovered our entrance to the exhibit would be marked for a specific time. That gave us ninety minutes to explore galleries I'd last visited on grammar school field trips, holding hands with my classmates as we gawked at Egyptian mummies and massive dinosaur skeletons.

Northern Flicker
Colaptes auratus

Warren and I headed left and discovered an area devoted to birds. Display case after display case contained the stuffed remains of thousands of species, ranging from the tiniest bee hummingbird—weighing slightly more than a dime—to the ostrich, a three-hundred-pound bird standing taller than me. Within minutes, I was transfixed by the intricate details, ravishing colors, brilliant design, limitless diversity, and even the hysterical hairdos of hundreds of feathered friends. I marveled at the architectural prowess of the long-tailed tailorbird, which crafts a nest out of a single leaf, using its fine, pointed bill as a needle and using cotton shreds, fine grass, or spider silk as string.

The northern flicker woodpecker has a four-inch tongue. Amazing! This bright red tongue is designed to extend deep into a tree to seek insects, yet when not in use, the tongue winds like a tape measure inside the woodpecker's

COMMON PEAFOWL
Pavo cristatus
L 40" (adult ♂ to 90")
Common in zoos; small feral populations exist in southern California.
Voice: Male gives very loud, wailing cries.

135

skull. I pondered the irony of the name *common peafowl* for an Indian pheasant with the most magnificent five-foot tail of green, purple, and black feathers woven into a pattern of stunning circles. There's nothing common about that bird! I laughed at the hoatzin, a goofy-looking creature with a wacky spiked haircut. And then there's the gorgeous pink-capped fruit dove, adorned entirely in green and yellow feathers except for its blazing pink head. I could go on and on.

What was intended as a gift about baseball for my husband serendipitously became an hour of worship for my Creator. Who is this Masterful Designer who imagined these creatures and poured out his ideas with such a mix of seemingly capricious, fanciful, glorious, hysterical, and yet deeply wise strokes of utter genius? I marveled at his power, brilliance, attention to the tiniest detail, and apparent delight in crafting over

9,300

species of birds that are often overlooked by humans and yet never escape their Creator's awareness. All I could say to myself was, **"Wow. Wow, wow, wow."**

It is one thing to exalt our God for the limitless wonder of his creative power. It is another thing altogether to realize that because we are made in God's image, our ability to

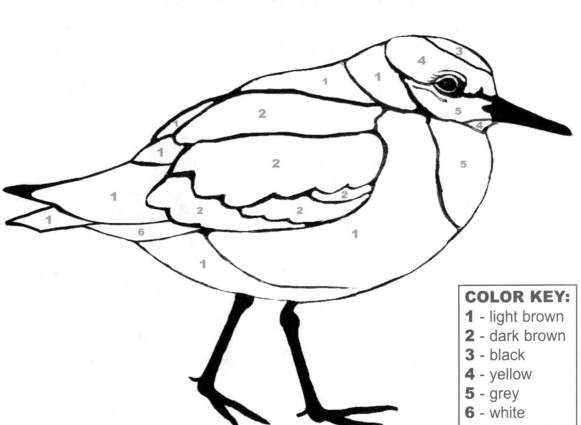

WHITE-THROATED SPARROW
PAINT BY NUMBERS

COLOR KEY:
1 - light brown
2 - dark brown
3 - black
4 - yellow
5 - grey
6 - white

Go ahead and copy! Permission is hereby granted to reproduce this page.

create is a direct reflection of the One who gave us life. In her classic book, *The Mind of the Maker*, author Dorothy Sayers asks: "How then can we be said to resemble God? . . . The characteristic common to God and [humans] is apparently. . . the desire and the ability to make things."

While we are incapable of making something out of nothing, every time we engage in the creative process we are like our Maker. James Romaine calls our creativity "a ringing echo of his image within us." What an inspiring thought— God must experience delight every time one of his children sweeps a brush across a blank canvas, taps out a new melody on a keyboard, or combines a sequence of steps on a dance floor. Artists are here and now extensions of the One who imagined every little bird's wing, who ushers the sun to its place every morning, and sustains a universe of galaxies so awesome we cannot begin to grasp its dimensions. When we create, we live out a large part of what it means to be human, to be crafted by a loving Father who intends for us to express ourselves as we make art. Creativity glorifies our God. In this chapter we explore the gift of creativity and why it matters so much in church. To begin, it's helpful to establish a fundamental understanding of just what creativity is and who can be called "creative."

What Is Creativity?

I don't know any artist who wouldn't light up with a smile at being described as "creative." The very word implies that a person has the ability to make something new, has a fresh perspective, a fertile imagination, and radical ideas or concepts. Essentially, creativity is a process of synthesis, and most of us readily recognize creativity when we see it. We delight in another's ability to see something in a unique way and sometimes wonder, "Why didn't *I* think of that?" Yet we carry around several deep-seated myths about the mystery of creativity. The most dangerous myth is that only certain people are blessed with this gift.

In *Orbiting the Giant Hairball*, writer and artist Gordon MacKenzie describes his frequent visits to grammar schools to speak to children. He often began by asking, "How many of you are artists?" When the audience was kindergarteners or children in early primary grades, every hand immediately shot up. The percentage declined to about half when he addressed children in the middle grades. By the time Gordon met with fifth and sixth graders, only a few students tentatively raised their hands. Gordon found this predictable pattern everywhere he went. How sad. All of us start out thinking of ourselves as little creative geniuses. But somewhere along the way, we apply those labels only to those we deem can "draw really good pictures." We then relegate ourselves to the larger part of the population who simply aren't very gifted in the creative realms.

Research refutes the myth that only a few humans should be characterized as "creative." Alex Osborn, author of *Your Creative Power*, doesn't let any of us off the hook when he emphatically states: "An analysis of almost all the psychological tests ever made points to the conclusion that creative talent is normally distributed—that all of us possess this talent. The difference is only in degree; and that degree is largely influenced by effort."

I don't know if these words inspire me or make me feel guilty! It's much easier to believe that creativity belongs only to a few gifted geniuses, so I can relax and make excuses when I lack creative power. On the other hand, if every one of us can, by intention and effort, increase our creative capacities, imagine how abundant our daily lives would be and how full of life our church services would become. *Every one of us possesses the God-given potential to become more creative.*

Creativity in Church

Many people have the impression that "creativity in church" is an oxymoron. They can't imagine a church service in which anything surprising, out of the ordinary, or even close to cutting edge might occur. Rather, many attend church on mental autopilot, predicting almost everything moments before it happens. This is why church has a reputation of being one of the most boring ways a person could spend an hour.

I long for people to drive away from the hour on Sunday saying, **"They kept my interest the whole time."** Our aim should be to create services so compelling, so

meaningful, and so unexpected, that the time sails by and attenders leave with an enthusiastic desire to talk about their experience as well as the content of the service. We want to ignite a "buzz" that propels them into the parking lot. Our children's ministry, Promiseland, aims to make Sunday morning the best hour of a kid's week—and in our main auditorium, we attempt to do the same for adults.

Yet there is a challenge. *Sundays come around with amazing regularity, every seven days!* On a weekly basis, those entrusted with planning creative services face a terrifyingly blank sheet of paper. It's extremely difficult to be truly creative fifty-two Sundays a year, to dig down deep for new ideas rather than relying on tried-and-true formulas. When I mentally scroll back through years of church services, some Sundays stand out because of a great idea, while others stand out because they languished in the dangerous land of entropy.

The Power of a Great Idea

We sat in a stuffy room with no windows, staring together at a blank sheet on a large flipchart. Once again our team faced the challenge of creating an Easter service. That glorious holiday comes around on an annual basis, and every year I wonder if we can come up with one more way to celebrate the Resurrection. Given the vacant looks on team members' faces, I wasn't too optimistic we would land on a radically awesome idea. Then Mark, our restless illustrator, started doodling on the flipchart as we threw around some preliminary concepts. Someone mentioned the idea of a bridge, with no clear sense of what we would do with a bridge. But Mark drew one anyway. (It gave him something to do while we stumbled around in the early, awkward phases of generating ideas.) Unfortunately, we closed the meeting two hours later with no greater definition of our Easter plan than when we began. It appeared we would simply have to start again at the next meeting.

Later that day I met with our pastor about another matter. He inquired about our morning meeting and how our Easter plans were coming along. I had to make a split-second decision about how much to say. I wondered if it was prudent to tell Bill about the bridge idea, since it really wasn't an idea at all but only an interesting image, and he might grab onto it, like it, and ask us to actually develop it—when in reality we had no clue what to do with the bridge. All that happened in my brain in a matter of seconds. I am not always very discerning with what I say. I told Bill about the bridge. And guess what? He loved it. I hastened to explain that we really didn't know where to go next, and we weren't sure what, if anything, it had to do with Easter. But he wanted to live with it awhile and see if he could use the bridge image as the foundation for his Easter message.

To make a long story short, the bridge idea catapulted from a doodle on a flipchart to the centerpiece of an entire service our congregation won't soon forget. The production team, displaying their typical enthusiasm and tendency to run ahead with a *big idea,* designed and built the mother of all bridges, almost spanning the width of our stage. Now we really had to use it! In the end, we wrote a drama sketch enacted on the bridge and choreographed a dance to portray the miraculous way Jesus Christ provides a bridge to God. Our pastor skillfully and passionately taught the congregation the truth that we cannot walk over the bridge ourselves; only by dropping our human efforts to pay for our sins and receiving the gift of grace can we walk to the other side, where a loving heavenly Father waits expectantly to welcome us home. All of these things made for a powerful service, but it wasn't until the services concluded that we began to see how God intended for the bridge to impact us with even more power than any of us could have imagined.

While our team gathered down front after the first of seven Easter services, we observed Bill walking over the bridge with a gentleman. They were taking their time and talking earnestly and quietly as they walked. It turns out that this man had approached our pastor after the service and asked if he could walk over the bridge as a symbol of his

new faith and of his desire to abandon human effort and to receive God's grace. Bill prayed with him and then together they traversed the bridge. In the services that followed, Bill related this story and invited anyone for whom walking over the bridge might be meaningful to stick around afterwards and do just that. To our amazement, hundreds of people lined up after each service. We witnessed old and young, married couples and single folks, Caucasians, Asians, African Americans, and Hispanics intently crossing that bridge. Some paused in the middle to pray. Others grasped the hand of a young child, and many had a bounce in their step and a twinkle in their eye. Grace will do that to you. And it all began with a simple image—an idea we didn't even recognize as wonderful until we played with it, brought it to life, and then watched as God took it beyond any of our wildest dreams. I will never get over the power of a great idea.

The Dangerous Land of Entropy

Unfortunately, there have been other services—even eras in our church—when creativity seemed elusive. We were stuck in a quagmire and desperately needed the fresh water of new thinking. *Entropy* is defined as "the degradation of matter and energy to an ultimate state of inert uniformity." Huh? I prefer to describe it as the time when things grow tired. We realize that no matter how effective, creative, and refreshing our ideas once seemed, they have now entered the land where almost everything eventually does—the place of the tired, worn out, over-used, and tightly-held ideas of the past. How I wish it were not so! Most of us are stunned by how quickly great communication approaches, styles, or forms begin to stagger and feel predictable. It seems like just yesterday we were celebrating the wonder of these new ideas and now they're already passé?

Years ago, we realized our weekend services had landed in a big-time rut. We had often put together what we call a "run" of art forms, usually including a dramatic sketch followed by a song, prayer, and comments from one of our pastors. These runs worked wonderfully for quite awhile until, like most things, they became precisely what attenders expected. They could have put the puzzle pieces of our service order together blindfolded if we'd asked them to.

Leaders, by their calling and make-up, are the ones who must spot and intercept entropy *early*, long before anyone else notices and the yawning commences. I haven't always awakened to entropy soon enough. If I dig deep to understand why, I can often trace this weakness to laziness or fear. Admitting something is tired requires leaders to initiate change, have difficult conversations, and enter into a long process of risk-taking and experimentation. It's far easier to look the other way longer than we should, to wait until most of the congregation has either gone to sleep in church or voted with their feet by simply staying home.

To avoid falling into entropy, we have learned to regularly ask questions such as these:

- Have we surprised our congregation lately?
- What could we do in this service that would be totally unexpected?
- Has the order of our service grown tired and predictable?
- What new art forms can we add to our toolbox to help us communicate truth?
- How can we combine art forms in fresh ways to breathe life into the service? For example, we could add visuals to music, combine video with drama, bring Scripture to life with multiple readers, or involve the congregation in interactive exercises and experiences.
- What special events—we call them "buzz events"—can we create to shake things up from our normal pattern? Buzz events might include bringing in guests to interview, guest artists, or turning the entire service over to one area, such as the student or children's ministry.
- What can we learn from what other churches are doing?

I'm convinced all of us would much prefer to be in a church where we experience great ideas far more than we experience entropy. This does not mean that churches have to jettison meaningful traditions. For example, we'd be risking mutiny at Willow Creek if we failed to end our Christmas Eve services by singing *Silent Night* together.

But some traditions can be revisited and even prepared in a new way so we hold onto that which is most meaningful while preventing it from dying a slow death. Churches built around a liturgical calendar and order of service can also commit to creative effort, discovering ways to communicate timeless truths with a variety of approaches. Avoiding entropy begins with nurturing both individual and team creativity—both are essential for crafting powerful church services.

Nurturing Individual Creativity

If I accept the idea that all of us have the potential to be creative and to be more creative today than we were yesterday, then I am responsible to develop my own creativity with intention and effort. As I sift through many experts' wise words and closely observe highly creative people, three traits stand out. Creative people are confident, curious, and courageous. Becoming a more creative person requires paying attention to how I can strengthen all three of these traits.

Confidence

This first characteristic sounds counter-intuitive. Many artistic people don't seem very confident; in fact, we often think of artists as insecure and full of self-doubt. But when it comes to creativity and idea generation, a self-fulfilling prophecy seems to be at work. When people have confidence that ideas exist and can be theirs for the taking, they actually are more creative. In his book *How to Get Ideas*, Jack Foster states:

> For the most part the difference between people who crackle with ideas and those who don't has little to do with some innate ability to come up with ideas. It has to do with the belief that they can come up with ideas. . . . Once you know that ideas exist and that you will find them, a great calm envelops you. It is a calm you need today more than ever.

Whenever I engage in the creative process, I need to look at my confidence level. Do I have faith ideas will come? Do I look at the . . .

blank sheet . . .

Present and in aWE!

of paper or the empty canvas and feel overcome by the negative internal voices scream-ing that there are simply no new ideas and I might as well give up before I begin? Or, do I resist and silence those voices and "take captive every thought to make it obedient to Christ" (2 Corinthians 10:5)? I must transform my mind to recognize that in God's universe there is an infinite quantity of ideas, and I can open up myself to receive and recognize the unlimited possibilities awaiting my discovery. We can be encouraged in our creative quests by remembering how great ideas have emerged in the past and trust-ing God's faithfulness to give us more than enough new ideas for today. This is a disci-pline of the mind that we must nurture.

Curiosity

Highly creative people are also ravenously curious. They accumulate diverse knowledge and experiences and are willing to constantly explore other outlooks. Creative people excel at listening and seeing. With childlike eyes, they explore and turn over and stand with wonder at life's smallest details, even those remote from their own interests. Addressing the topic of writing itself, author Anne Lamott captures this spirit in *Bird by Bird*:

> I honestly think in order to be a writer, you have to learn to be reverent.... Let's think of rever-ence as awe, as presence in and openness to the world.... This is our goal as writers, I think; to help others have this sense of— please forgive me—wonder, of seeing things anew, things that can catch us off guard, that break in on our small, bordered worlds. When this happens, everything feels more spacious. Try walking around with a child who's going, "Wow, wow! Look at that dirty

dog! Look at that burned-down house! Look at that red sky!" And the child points and you look, and you see, and you start going, "Wow! Look at that huge crazy hedge! Look at that teeny little baby! Look at the scary dark cloud!" I think this is how we are supposed to be in the world—present and in awe.

Present and in awe. To pay attention. As creative people, we must break out of our habits, learn to look and to listen, and build up the storehouse of our minds with extraneous bits of information and discoveries we can assemble one day in ways we cannot yet know. Louis Pasteur once said, "Chance favors only the prepared mind." To nurture curiosity, we need to travel more, visit unusual places, read like crazy, ask probing questions, imitate a little child and ceaselessly ask, "Why?" Getting out of our ruts and rubbing shoulders with different people in different places will refresh our creative spirits and surprise us with new ideas.

Courage

The third trait common to highly creative people is courage. New ideas and fresh actions require risk. Few moments are more frightening than when we take a deep breath and offer up a new perspective. Everything in us feels tentative, vulnerable, afraid that what we are about to say is the stupidest thing anyone has ever thought of, and certainly within seconds it will be shot down by a wiser team member who will judge us for our obvious insanity. But whether we are creating alone—and need to drown out inner voices of judgment—or brainstorming with a team, fighting through the temptation to retread or bury our unborn ideas, we must wage this courageous fight. It takes courage to break down boundaries. It takes courage to admit when we are stuck. And I believe it takes courage for artists to use their art in a church setting.

Nurturing courage simply requires us to let go. Gordon MacKenzie lists what we must be willing to release:

> **Let go of the strategies that have worked for us in the past . . .**
> **Let go of our biases, the foundation of our illusions . . .**
> **Let go of our grievances, the root source of our victimhood . . .**
> **Let go of our so-often-denied fear of being found unlovable.**

Gordon then reminds us that this letting go is an ongoing process, every day of our lives, if we hope to keep our creative spirits alive.

If you provide leadership to artists, you need to help team members grow in confidence, curiosity, and courage. Helping artists to assess which of these traits most require their attention and development will stoke their creative contribution over time.

Nurturing Team Creativity

Much of the creative activity in church work involves artists crafting and developing their ideas in solitude. But there is another dimension to creativity—the team process. A leader of artists entrusted with creating powerful church services is only effective if he or she develops a creative culture—an environment in which teams are empowered and inspired to generate great ideas together. I've spent over twenty-five years attempting to learn how to get the most out of a group of artists without destroying their spirits in the process. It's a tricky business. I make lots of mistakes and learn along the way. Nurturing the creativity of healthy teams requires us to make it fun, lead brainstorming well, know when to stop, and make room for failure.

Make it Fun

David Ogilvy, leader of a highly respected advertising agency, once said, "When people aren't having any fun they seldom produce good advertising." The same could be said about those who create church services. We tend to get weighed down by the serious nature of what we do, always aware that what we produce might make the difference in someone's eternity. But if we make the creative process too serious, we greatly diminish our team's childlike imagination. Because our team must create every single week, and often more than once a week, we must find ways to make this experience more an adventure than a burden.

So how do we make it fun? I'm sure there are as many possibilities as there are churches, but here are a few things I've learned.

Fd:

I don't know why, but having snacks and the promise of hot coffee or iced tea just seems to make it all more fun.

Place:

It also matters where a creative team meets—though I admit much of our brainstorming takes place in windowless rooms that could use decorating. We try to make up for drab locations with childlike toys, such as a soft ball, and with warm lighting and comfortable seating. Weather permitting (which includes maybe seven days in Chicago), we'll head outside and breathe fresh air. I've often captured small teams and taken them to a local restaurant or a private home just to change things up a bit.

Laughter:

Most of all, I encourage teams to laugh a lot. Even though we steward weighty responsibilities, we must lean into one another's humor. Begin the creative session with lighthearted talk about the latest hot movie, an experience with your children, or a funny thing that happened at the grocery store. Show me a team who laughs a lot, and I'll bet they consistently come up with truly creative ideas.

Lead Brainstorming Effectively

To brainstorm means using the brain to storm a creative problem. A team—ideally five to ten individuals—gathers for a couple hours to attack the creation of a new event or church service. My best resource for learning how to effectively lead such meetings is *A Whack on the Side of the Head*, by Roger von Oech. Years ago, that book gave our team an understanding of how to manage the unwieldy, often uncomfortable, process of creating something together. Mr. Von Oech's book added several terms to our vocabulary, such as *phases of brainstorming*, *umbrella of mercy*, and *stepping stones*.

Phases of brainstorming. We learned that there are two phases of brainstorming—the highly imaginative phase when we play with ideas and the practical phase when we shape and define our ideas. In the first phase, we aim for a huge quantity of ideas. In von Oech's words: "Quantity, quantity, and more quantity! This is the surest recipe for ideas. The odds are that only a few of the many ideas we hit upon will be any good. Therefore, the more alternatives we think up, the better our chance of success . . . the best ideas seldom come first."

We don't allow anyone to judge ideas in the imaginative phase—in fact, the wilder the ideas the better.

Umbrella of mercy. Team members all feel shaky in offering a new idea, especially if they think others might consider it a little wacky. Observers of our creative meetings are mystified when they see one of our artists put a hand over his or her head just before communicating a possible idea. This is visual shorthand at Willow for requesting the umbrella of mercy. It's our code for grace giving and lack of judgment. If a team member puts on a critic's hat, we literally throw a ball—a soft one—at that person to

PATH

TO

A

remind us all that now is not the time to judge or evaluate. This is because of the power of association.

Stepping stones. Any idea, no matter how wacky, might be just the ticket that leads someone else to the next great idea. We learned that these ideas are called *stepping stones.* They are enormously valuable because they propel us forward to something that can work. After we've assembled lots and lots of ideas, we give ourselves permission to shift into the practical phase. This is where we get more realistic about our resources—deadlines, personnel, cost, etc. We try to maintain a positive, can-do attitude even in this practical phase.

The leader of the brainstorming meeting must promote and protect the culture—always encouraging the spirit of risk-taking, frowning on the critics, and yet moving the team toward getting something done. We can't dream all day about options that are truly unaffordable or inappropriate. Guiding the team toward that which is doable while maintaining optimism and joy is quite a challenge. A big part of nurturing team creativity is knowing when it's time to quit pushing.

GREAT

Know When to Stop

When individuals or teams get stuck, sometimes we must persevere. But there comes a point when that track becomes fruitless, when it's time to take a break and breathe different air. Have you ever noticed how many fabulous ideas emerge in the car or shower? Experts say this is because when we choose to turn our attention to something else, the very act of stepping away and relaxing may evoke creative inspiration. Leaders of artists must learn how to "read a room." If every face on the

IDEA

team is lifeless and begging for mercy, it's time to give it a rest!
(As Gordon MacKenzie said, "Get those cows off the milking machine.")

Team creativity is one of the most precious commodities
any church has. Unfortunately, far too many organizations have come
to expect creativity at an unsustainable pace. Stanford University's Jeffrey Pfeffer calls
companies that fail to effectively manage their people "toxic":

See page 80.

> It requires people to choose between having a life and having a career.
> A toxic company says to people, "We want to own you. We're going to put
> you in a situation where you have to work in a style and on a pace that is
> not sustainable. We want you to come in here and burn yourself out—and
> then you can leave."

I fear that his description may also apply to some churches—or to the team I lead. I
must protect these treasured creative men and women so they can keep contributing
with enthusiasm, health, and joy. Leaders, I urge you to know when it's time to stop, to
give your people a break, to come up with an alternative approach for a few services
every year, so the hearts of your creative team members can flourish.

Make Room for Failure

Microsoft believes that to manage creativity we must "hire smart people who think"
and then "expect employees to fail." When smart
people take risks, there will be occasional train
wrecks. Every good

company and every prevailing church has scrapbooks of stories describing their biggest bloopers. We are no exception. But as a church grows, as the stakes seem to get higher every Sunday and we see the wonder of life change, a corresponding fear of failure descends. We can become so bound by fear of mistakes that we no longer venture into the unknown. Artists do their work with one part braced for a bruising if all does not go well. Trying to meet rising expectations for "better," "more powerful," or "more creative" services creates a culture of fear and kills creative spirit.

There is no learning without failure. All of us know that. Yet we still hope to be the exception, to soar to new heights without the valleys of error. The perspective of thirty years in ministry has given me the ability to see how well some creative failures have served us. Long ago in a brainstorming meeting, we got pumped up about designing a baptism service focused on the scripture about the names of God's children being written in a book of life. Our visual artists created a large book for the stage, with space for each person being baptized to write his or her name. We pictured a powerful moment as the names were written down and prepared music and a drama sketch to support the theme. But it all fell flat. The great moment never really happened. Baptism was held up by lines of people waiting to sign their names. The metaphor lacked the vitality we envisioned. At the end of that day, I still gave us an "A" for trying something new. Years later, we chuckle at our book of life and remember that energetic brainstorming doesn't always deliver the outcome we imagine.

One way to test our ideas, especially for major church events, is to do a pilot for a small group of discerning people. This is akin to a Broadway play staging a pre–New York run in a small town like Poughkeepsie or a television program screening an episode with a small test market audience. Our team prepares a rough script and assembles music and other elements in the early phases of development and then invites key church leaders to a read-through.

happy dance

Afterwards, we ask for their feedback over coffee on how we can improve our material.

If something in the Sunday service clearly doesn't work, how we respond to failure matters big time. Assuming the artists and teams all did their best—which is the first thing to explore—we must not shame people for taking risks. Never accuse artists that someone's eternity might be forever altered because of the failure. If we foster a culture of fear, we can truly say good-bye to any innovations for next week. Instead, in a loving, truthful manner, explore what can be learned and always give a pat on the back to anyone who went out on a limb and tried something new. Over time, it's obviously our goal to decrease our failure rate and to take calculated risks because of all we have learned. But we'll never be able to say good-bye to failure altogether if we choose to aim for creativity. It's part of the deal.

As leaders make room for fun, lead brainstorming effectively, know when to stop pushing, and allow for failure, the culture of creativity will flourish in our churches. And ideas will flow. . . .

I'll Never Get Over it

As long as I live, I'll never get over the wonder that God made me to be a maker and that he longs to fill me with ideas. Jack Foster describes the experience this way:

happy dance

> There's nothing quite like it. You're sitting in a room trying to come up with an idea, a solution, a way to go, and nothing is happening, and there is nothing there but walls and barriers and closed doors and stop signs and dead ends, and you're frustrated and worried and wondering if you'll ever find a way out of this maze, this box, this trap, when all of a sudden it hits, and wham—you see the whole thing, all at once, solved, with everything fitting and working together. Whee.

happy dance

I could never count how many times I've sat alone facing a blank computer screen or joined a team of comrades in creative battle to brainstorm a service together. And whenever that idea hits, when the "whee" moment happens and you know it down to your toes, there's nothing to do but celebrate and do a happy dance.

We are limited human beings who often wrestle with voices that say there are no more ideas and we can't create. But we serve a God who is the Master Designer, the one who crafted every bird's intricate wing, who loves our churches more than we ever can. He has no limits, no creative end, no roadblocks. We have access to the Creator of All. For reasons I don't understand, he chooses to whisper ideas to the listening ones, to give us the manna we need for this day in this moment, if only we'll believe it and receive.

Thank you Father, for the privilege of being one who creates. May I choose to trust, to pay attention, and to move boldly with courage toward every blank sheet of paper you send my way. It's an honor to be crafted in your image.

Questions to Explore

1. How would you rate the overall creativity of your church? Do you celebrate the power of many great ideas, or are you dangerously close to the land of entropy? On what evidence do you base your assessment?

2. Three traits describe highly creative people—confidence, curiosity, and courage. Which of the three traits is the strongest for you personally? Why do you think this is your strongest trait? In which trait do you most need to grow? What specific steps can you take to nurture your own creativity?

3. How high is the fun factor when your team creates together? What can you do to make your creative culture more fun?

4. Assess how well your team honors the two phases of brainstorming—the highly imaginative, playful phase and the practical phase. How might you gather a greater quantity of ideas without premature judgment and criticism?

5. List three to five words that describe your culture when it comes to failure. What is the usual response? How might you establish a stronger atmosphere of learning, risk-taking, and growth?

chapter **ten**

If I had
to choose
just one
supreme
value,
I'd pick
authenticity
over
excellence
and creativity
simply because
the door to
attenders'
hearts and
minds will
slam shut the
instant they
pick up on
pretense of
any kind.

"This article will make your heart ache," said my friend John as he handed me a piece from GQ magazine. My friend was right—my heart sank as I read it. The article was written by Walter Kirn, a novelist and GQ's literary editor, who chose to examine the evangelical Christian subculture from the perspective of an outsider. For seven days Kirn immersed himself in the evangelical lifestyle. He listened only to music by Christian artists, watched only Christian videos, and even began each day with a "holy workout" inspired by a Christian book. Kirn's experiences and his perceptions of those who bear the name of Christ were scathing. On day seven, these words summed up his experiment:

[Evangelical Christianity] is mall Christianity. It's been malled. It's the upshot of some decision that to compete with them—to compete with 'N Sync and *Friends* and Stephen King and Matt and Katie and Abercrombie and Fitch and Jackie Chan and AOL and *Sesame Street*—the faithful should turn from their centuries-old tradition of fashioning transcendent art and literature and passionate folk forms such as gospel music. . . and instead head down to Tower or Blockbuster and check out what's selling, then try to rip it off, on a budget if possible and by employing artists who are either so devout or so plain desperate that they'll work for scale. What makes the stuff so half-assed, so thin, so weak and cumulatively so demoralizing. . . has nothing to do with faith. The problem is lack of faith.

Once again I felt sad, defensive, and even angry that people bearing the name *Christian* would be described with such *negative* **WORDS**. Now we can rant and rave and say that the writer must have visited all the wrong places and checked out all the wrong media sources to arrive at his conclusions. Surely if he had come to our church and met our friends, his experience would have been vastly different. But the point is that his perceptions and even his expectations as he ventured into the Christian community are commonly held by far too many people outside our faith. **The tragic truth is this: the reputation of evangelical Christians among people far from God is that we are** **greedy, narrow-minded, lifeless, simplistic, sneaky, and definitely not a part of the real world.** These assumptions damage the kingdom of God and prevent many people from taking even the first steps to investigate the truths of Christianity. Many folks lump it all together in their minds—Christian media, Christian individuals, and also the church. Their impressions of INAUTHENTICITY bleed from one category to the next.

Those of us planning church services face a huge uphill battle. New people often come to church starting from a negative, cynical position—they're not even neutral! The question we must grapple with is, What do people discover when they visit our churches, starting with the hour on Sunday? I want people to drive away from our church saying to one another, "Those people are real."

Authenticity is a core value that makes up for weaknesses elsewhere. If I had to choose just one supreme value, I'd pick authenticity over excellence and creativity simply because the door to attenders' hearts and minds will slam shut the instant they pick up on pretense of any kind. On the other hand, when people sense that the communicators and the environment are filled with integrity, they are far more forgiving if we aren't quite where we want to be with other values. So how do we ensure that our churches are perceived as the real deal? Authenticity begins with authentic people. Then we must pay attention to ensuring authenticity in our content and approach.

187

During services I typically sit to the far right in the second row of what we call the *bullpen.* I sit behind the pastors and producer who play key roles in the service (unless I'm teaching myself). Recently, I moved up to the front row to support a guest speaker. In the few moments before he went up to teach, I discerned that this man was someone I would love to have for a friend. He was warm, kind, funny, and very approachable. He didn't seem overly impressed with himself, even though within moments he would deliver a powerful message that rocked our congregation and was widely distributed with the release of hundreds of tapes. After the service, I talked with other members of our staff, all of whom had similar, positive responses—we wished he was on our team or that we could move to his town and serve with him!

My first impressions of our guest stemmed from an inner gauge I call my *authenticity meter.* Most of us utilize such a gauge, even if we're not completely aware of it. Within moments of meeting anyone, we assess whether this is a person we can relate to, someone we can trust. Those authenticity meters are functioning every time attenders visit our churches on Sunday mornings. From the ushers who welcome them, to the children's ministry and volunteers who care for their children, all the way to every person who participates in the service itself, people are checking us out. For those who haven't attended church in a long time, the incoming bias

not-so-normal
guy from page 64

may be that Christians will be anything but authentic. What are the characteristics of authentic people that result in our gauges reading "real"? Although it's not easy to nail down what makes us perceive that a person is genuine, I find myself looking for someone who consistently exhibits normalcy, humility, and honesty.

Normalcy

In chapter three, I described the need for casting normal people to communicate in our services. I'd like to develop this concept a little further. After all, defining the parameters of normal sounds dangerous and extremely tricky! And when we look at some leaders and prophets described in Scripture—from Isaiah preaching naked, to John the Baptist eating locusts in the wilderness—we see behavior that challenged the status quo and delivered a wake-up call to the listeners. Obviously, there are times when our sovereign God chooses to deliver his messages in unconventional ways. But most of the time, I contend that our effectiveness in communication often begins when listeners feel they can relate to those delivering the message.

"and this weekend we will be collecting winter coats for the poor."

is that a tiara on her head?

What seems normal to one person may be outside the bounds for another. It's not easy to define normal, but all of us know it when we see *abnormal*. Have you ever experienced a worship leader who changes his voice into a

"God voice"

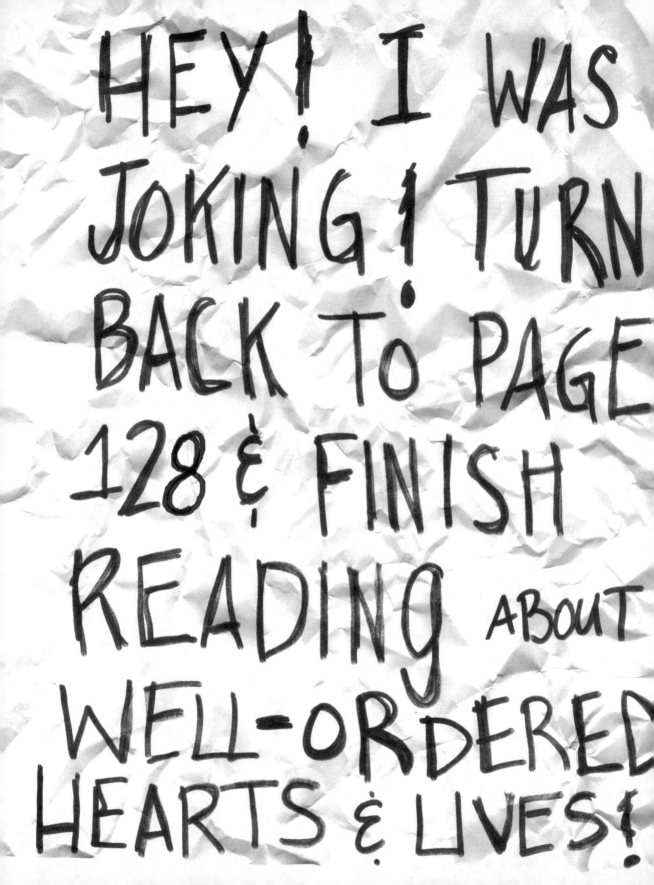

whenever he invites others to sing? Have you observed Christians speaking with a super sweet tone as they spout off clichés and oversimplify truth? Have you seen people on church platforms dress in ways that unnecessarily call attention to themselves instead of wearing clothing or jewelry that would be considered appropriate, contemporary, and normal to others?

People have a difficult time receiving truth if their walls go up because they discern that the person up front is a little goofy, bizarre, or just plain out of touch. We may wish this were not so and decide that people just need to be more tolerant, *or* we can accept commonly held principles of communication that underscore how essential it is for listeners to connect with the person delivering the message. In his classic book *The Mind Changers*, Dr. Em Griffin emphatically states that "persuasion rises or falls on the credibility of the speaker." As crass as it may sound, it's important that we like the people up front in our church services; that we could actually imagine having a cup of coffee with them and getting to know them better. Normalcy matters.

When we worship in the hour on Sunday, it's important to understand how people far from God might react to what they experience. What may be very normal to us or to our tradition may seem strange or even bizarre to them—whether we follow a serene liturgy or engage in more expressive worship. Most non-churched adults don't sing anywhere in public other than maybe the national anthem at a sporting event. They aren't familiar with church music or with how to behave in church. Sensitivity to the visitor does not mean discouraging believers from engaging in authentic worship. In fact, observing genuine Christians connecting with God can draw seekers toward longing to know and experience that connection for themselves. It may mean, however, that we adjust our worship expression if we hope to include people outside the faith. Coach believers to be aware that some attenders may not yet know Christ, and they may need to reserve some behaviors for settings that are exclusive to Christians.

These are extremely challenging decisions—unique to each community of faith—requiring tremendous discernment. The Apostle Paul provided guidelines for the church in Corinth, as their gatherings included both believers and unbelievers. His bottom line counsel was, "Everything should be done in a fitting and orderly way" (1 Corinthians 14:40).

I urge church leaders to frequently assess whether visitors coming on Sunday will walk away sensing that the Christians they observed are normal.

Humility

A vocalist walks up to sing a song on Sunday morning. She is dressed attractively and smiles warmly through-out the musical intro-duction. Once she opens her mouth, all who listen agree she has a beautiful voice—on pitch, rich tone, great dynamic range. At a few key moments, the vocalist soars and produces a few licks that leave her listeners in awe. But something is not right. Something intangible does not ring true. The content of the song is not connecting and several listeners begin to tune out or look away. What's the problem? Within moments, the authenticity meters go off in alarm. Most discerning people in the room conclude that this young woman is highly impressed with herself. She seems to be displaying vocal gymnastics for the sole purpose of wowing the audience. There is nothing genuine in her eyes. It's all about her. It's a performance.

The fundamental difference between perform-ance and ministry boils down to humility. No fruit of the Spirit is more essential to authenticity than a humble heart. Most of us can tell rather quickly whether an artist is all about the communication of truth and serving the Lord or all about herself. Yet humility, unlike the other godly traits we strive to attain, is a tricky one to pursue—if only because if we think we're making progress, we worry that now we're prideful! Humility is one of those virtues never gained by seeking it. The more we pursue it, the more it eludes us. It's awkward to try to make yourself more humble. The more obsessed with humility we become, the more we focus on ourselves—which was the problem in the first place. Before we explore this trait, it's important to be clear about what humility is not.

The Marks of Humility

Imagine a humble individual. Are you picturing a passive, weak, quiet, somber, self-deprecating doormat of a person? Keith Miller writes,

"I was taught that being humble was acting as if I were unimportant, inadequate, of no value. I got the idea that it was an outward attitude of 'I'm lucky to be here breathing good air when other more worthy people could have it!'"

Let's be clear from the start: Humility is *not* self-contempt.

← instead of folding down the corners of pages you want to mark, create your very own AN HOUR ON SUNDAY bookmark! turn to page 265 for instructions.

We all know people with a habit of putting themselves down and deflecting compliments. Ken Davis, a gifted Christian speaker, tells the story of going up to a vocalist after a church service to thank her for her song and how much it ministered to him. Her response was, "Oh, it wasn't me. It was God!" Ken was left feeling unheard and a little confused—he really did think she had sung the song! Some of us, in a misguided effort to receive praise with a humble spirit, end up discounting the appreciation of those who simply want to thank us. I love the way C.S. Lewis puts it:

Quote:

Do not imagine that if you meet a really humble man he will be what most people call "humble" nowadays; he will not be a sort of. . . person who is always telling you that, of course, he is nobody. Probably all you will think about him is that he seemed a cheerful, intelligent chap who took a real interest in what *you* said to *him*. If you do dislike him, it will be because you feel a little envious of anyone who seems to enjoy life so easily. He will not be thinking about humility: he will not be thinking about himself at all.

One cannot be humble and overly self-focused at the same time. Those who serve behind the scenes have a little easier time practicing humility than those whose gifts are more often in the spotlight. Unfortunately, some people who attend church apply star treatment to worship leaders, teachers, actors, vocalists, and others they frequently see up front. This kind of treatment makes it even more difficult for artists to maintain humility.

I recently experienced an awkward moment at a fast-food drive-through window. My daughter and I had stopped for a quick burger. A perky teenage girl took our order from the voice box. When I pulled up to the window to pay for our food, the order taker looked at me and inquired nervously, "Are you Nancy Beach?" I responded, and then she disappeared for what seemed like a long time to get my change. When she returned, this young woman was incredibly nervous as she handed me the money. "I'm sorry," she said. "I just had to go tell my manager. I feel like I'm waiting on a celebrity."

Of course my own teenager rolled her eyes. To her, I'm just Mom, and could we please get on with lunch! Like others on the Willow staff, I experience these encounters periodically. It's difficult when church attenders feel like they know you because they hear your stories and see you on the platform week after week. This happens in both large and small churches, in metropolitan areas and rural communities. How do we practice humility when some people treat us like we're better than the average person? How do we keep the focus off ourselves and stop believing our own press?

Humility can best be defined as seeing ourselves accurately. We are told in Romans 12:3 to not think more highly of ourselves than we should, but "think of yourself with sober judgment." Sober judgment requires facing the truth about our imperfections and having the wisdom to accept those limitations. But it also means having an accurate view of our gifts, recognizing that none of us deserve or even asked for the gifts we have—our Creator assigned them. If we've been entrusted with a high level of giftedness, that should lead us to sober-mindedness and responsibility, not pride. Luke 12:48 often echoes in my mind, challenging me to carefully steward my gifts: "Much is required from those to whom much is given, and much more is required from those to whom much more is given" (NLT).

A humble person is actually a very free person, because the need for pretense is diminished. Humility sets us free to fully express ourselves, to delight in who God made us to be, to resign from the constant competition to be better than everyone else. G.K. Chesterton wrote, "It is always the secure who are humble." Humility is not for the weak; we need the strength of humility to reach our greatest heights.

Curing Pride Attacks

Humility is throwing oneself away in complete concentration on someone or something else. If you've struggled with pride—I have—I encourage you to take up two challenges that have helped me greatly. First, look upward and then look outward. Looking upward means focusing on the One who is immeasurably superior to us in every respect. The more we truly seek God and focus on his attributes—absolute holiness, wisdom, compassion, power—the less tempted we are to think too highly of ourselves. Joe Stowell writes, "Humility is a by-product of being consumed with Christ's supremacy. When we are enthralled with all Christ is, we begin naturally to display . . . humility." Seeing God with vivid clarity results in viewing myself with sober judgment. I'm no longer overly impressed with who I am or what I accomplish.

Looking outward simply means turning our attention to the needs of others. The spiritual discipline of secret service is the best way I know to cure a pride

The discipline of secrecy will help us break the grip of human opinion over our souls and our actions.

attack, especially for those who are often up front. When we engage in hidden acts of kindness, a deep change begins to occur in our spirits. Dallas Willard writes, "The discipline of secrecy will help us break the grip of human opinion over our souls and our actions." Our natural tendencies are certainly not to serve in hidden ways. We long to let our actions be known in order to receive honor and recognition. In fact, some of us devise subtle ways to call attention to what we have done, somehow slipping and letting others know about our heroic, "hidden" service. We must defeat this temptation and serve others primarily because our service delights the heart of God and strengthens our character. Serving the under-resourced, the sick, the elderly, the disabled, or those in prison has a way of dramatically altering our obsession with self and our own agenda. The more we enroll in the school of secret service, the more we will find the grace of humility slip in upon us unawares.

But just a word for those of us who use our gifts up front. When you walk up on that platform, do not hold back in a misguided attempt to be humble. If you sing, allow yourself to become so completely absorbed in the content that you give the song all you've got. The same holds true for teachers, instrumentalists, actors, and dancers. Humility is not inconsistent with excellence and passion. Go for it—all the way—and pour out your gift with all your heart, knowing that the God who blessed you with that gift is thrilled to see you soar as the kingdom is advanced.

So what does it mean for church artists to be clothed with humility as we enter the hour on Sunday? Fundamentally it means recognizing that it's not all about me. It's not about . . .

what I need in rehearsal

how much I am appreciated

whether I feel good about everything

how I come across

how I look

others treat me

Even if others treat you like it *is* all about you, fill your mind with the scripture that teaches: "Do nothing out of selfish ambition or vain conceit. Rather, in humility value others above yourselves, not looking to your own interests but each of you to the interests of the others" (Philippians 2:3–4).

Sundays would be so awesome if each of us genuinely looked out more for the interests of others than for our own: if the music director humbly sought to serve the sound engineer; if the actor treated the production team with dignity; if the video team was concerned with a vocalist's needs; if the pastor showed up to encourage others more than to be admired by others. Our churches could be places where each person, both on and off the platform, focuses on others, performing hidden acts of service and finding ways for fellow team members to shine. Leaders within the arts ministry must be willing to initiate difficult conversations with any team member who displays a consistent prideful spirit. Without humility, authenticity is impossible.

Honesty

Lights come up on an office scene. An actor portraying a businessman is startled late at night by a fellow worker, a woman also working overtime. The man enthusiastically announces that he just closed a major deal, one that will bring quite a pay-off to the company and certainly add to his own prestige. The woman joins him in celebration, claiming that she was at the office at 8:30 on a Friday night working on a proposal. As the scene progresses, we detect something in the air. The man asks the woman why a competent, attractive person like her would be at the office when she could be out having fun. She responds by asking, "So you find me attractive?"

"That's a no-brainer," the guy answers. Just when things begin to heat up, a janitorial worker interrupts to take out the trash. The businessman notices a phone message and quickly makes a call. We listen as he checks in with his family, who are visiting relatives out of town—a wife, who clearly does not respond with excitement to news of the big deal he just made, and T.J., his young son. Now we know what's at stake. The guy hangs up the phone, and the flirtation continues. He will not have family waiting for him at home tonight. The man and the woman raise their glasses to toast.

When the lights fade, we wonder where the evening will end. Clearly they are at a crossroads, on a precipice that could lead to disaster.

We've all been there, right at that edge. If it's not sexual temptation it could be a decision about ethics, stealing, lying, greed, or any other sin. But at that moment in church we faced, with brutal honesty, the fragile place all of us find ourselves when we choose between

light or DARKNESS.

The dramatic scene confronted us with the raw truth about our vulnerability to disobedience and prepared us to hear about the way out that only God provides.

There can be no authenticity without honesty. People who sit in our churches on Sunday morning are waiting to see if we will simply tell them the truth—the truth about life, about struggle and pain, about the mess in this world, and about our own shaky experiences. They also need to hear the truth about ultimate hope. But first we must admit that we understand trouble, that none of us is exempt from trials and temptation, and that we know life is difficult. If Christians sugarcoat the truth or try to hide, escaping the reality of what everyone else clearly sees, we will be perceived as out of touch. **Church is not the place for pretense or platitudes. It's the place for telling the truth.** The truth includes the amazing message of unbelievable grace, offered to all who earnestly seek God. Those of us who are members of God's family must not paint ourselves as any better than those far from the Father—we are simply recipients of amazing grace.

A theater professor once taught me that when watching a dramatic scene, a director must keep asking two key questions: "Do I believe this? If not, what is keeping me from believing it?" That counsel has served me well not only when assessing a theatrical piece, but also when looking at an entire church service. When I observe music, teaching, video, drama, or any other part of the hour on Sunday, do I believe it down to my toes—or is something getting in my way of trusting what is being communicated? We do not serve attenders well if we think it's best to ignore reality, to pretend that Christians don't struggle with parenting, marriage, ethics in the workplace, financial challenges, anger, lust, guilt, pride, greed, loneliness, and fear of failure. Rather, we need to *identify* with the realities of the human condition and with the world we all live in Monday through Saturday. Perhaps no tool can communicate honesty more effectively than a story can.

1. DO I BELIEVE THIS?
2. IF NOT, WHAT IS KEEPING ME FROM BELIEVING IT?

When attenders hear a real-life story—whether from a teacher, fellow attender, through a drama, video, or song—they sense undeniable truth. We frequently ask individuals from our congregation to tell their stories in a service. The person doesn't have to be eloquent or polished. In fact, the congregation seems to root for those who are most afraid as they begin to speak. Our team works with the storytellers in advance to edit their pieces to the most essential details. We've heard stories of family reconciliations, struggles with drug and alcohol addictions, coming to faith through an arrest, and a young Jewish woman who accepted Jesus as her Messiah. Some stories are more dramatic than others, but all of them fully engage the listeners just because they are so achingly true. Often the person ends by simply stating, "And that's my story." The audience members, who have sat riveted for four or five minutes, often leap to their feet in applause and support of these courageous, honest storytellers. There's something powerful about simple truth telling!

Honesty also comes through when vocalists introduce songs with brief personal remarks. On occasion we've even asked actors to break out of character at the conclusion of a drama scene and describe the actual life experience that led to writing that script. In one service, just before a powerful dance piece, we showed a video of the dancer in her real life as a mom and a relatively new follower of Christ. These windows into the everyday worlds of artists deepen the power of the artistic elements and dismantle the wall that often separates attenders from those up front. Driving home from the hour on Sunday, whether or not they yet agree with all they heard, attenders can at least say, "Those people are real."

The value of authenticity is impossible to attain unless we begin with authentic communicators. Yet, even if the folks on our platforms are the real deal, it's possible for parts of our services to be perceived as inauthentic. Why? It comes down to the content or our approach. Therefore, our next area of exploration is the creation and preparation of *Transcendent Moments.*

Questions to Explore

1. Think of someone on your team who comes across as the real deal to people in your church. Describe what it is about that person that reads as authentic.

2. How would you rate the most frequent communicators at your church on normalcy, humility, and honesty? Where do you see the most opportunity for growth?

3. Evaluate whether your Sunday service content addresses life's pain and difficulties. What picture of the Christian experience are you painting for the people sitting in your congregation? Does that picture match reality? How can you paint a more accurate picture while still offering the hope of Christ?

chapter **eleven**

I believe
the potential
for moments
that matter
exists in
every church,
as we listen
for God's
guidance,
develop
our crafts,
and pray like
crazy for
supernatural
power to be
unleashed.

Fifteen years ago, four of us sat on the edge of our seats in the tenth row, anticipating a wonderful Holy Week service at another church in another state. I vividly recall our excitement about this unique opportunity to gain new ideas and inspiration. The stunning auditorium and incredible stage sets told us right away that this church had a budget way out of our league. We couldn't wait to see what they'd do with their state-of-the-art lighting, sound, costumes, and staging. Over the next two hours, we watched as the story of Passion Week was dramatized at a production level far beyond anything we'd yet attempted.

As we headed back to the hotel that night, our team was uncharacteristically quiet. At first I chalked it up to the long day of travel and a bit of jet lag. But I didn't feel much like talking either. None of us wanted to criticize the efforts of another church by expressing our disappointment. We had deep respect for all the preparation, rehearsal hours, and sacrifice of so many staff and volunteers. And yet, we were left feeling . . . well, not feeling much. Finally, one of us broke the silence and said, "I was just hoping for a moment. I was awed by all they did technically, but, honestly, I was never moved." That made us all very sad. We know what it's like to create services or special events with the best intentions but, in the end, conclude there was no moment of transcendence.

Moments are tricky to define. I often say, "You simply know when you've had one." Moments occur in our everyday lives, often catching us unaware. Bringing tears to the eyes, a lump in the throat, a catch of breath, or a belly laugh from the gut. Buechner writes, "Our lives are a series of moments, and life itself is grace." The purpose of this chapter is to explore moments that can happen in church, times when the Spirit of God breaks through, and people walk out saying, "I was moved." Certainly there is a degree of subjectivity when we consider moments—one person may be deeply affected by a Sunday experience that barely registers with another. But there are occasions when the majority can't deny something significant is happening, that a supernatural God thing is going on. That's why we describe such moments as transcendent.

I experienced a few significant moments in the church of my youth. One standout took place when a guest artist ministered at a Sunday evening service. (Yes, I endured many of those!) As a young teen, I'd never heard of Ken Medema. That night he sat down alone at the keyboard in front of our church, and I was captivated from the first note to the last. I'd never heard a musician in church tell such riveting stories through song and speak directly to my heart. At times I felt I was the only person in the room; it seemed Ken's music projected from the stage straight to me in the balcony.

Like most teens, I was trying to determine how to invest my one and only life, wondering if God would ever use me to make any difference. Ken's lyrics pierced my soul:

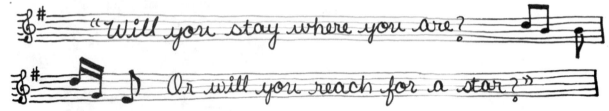

"Will you stay where you are? Or will you reach for a star?"

The Holy Spirit dug around inside of me, prompting me to trust my heavenly Father, to take more risks, to begin a journey of listening to God and seeking to find my place in the kingdom. That moment marked me. I knew something supernatural was going on and that I would never be the same.

As limited human beings, we can only prepare for the potential of moments—the transcendent, supernatural anointing is beyond our control. There are human and spiritual dimensions involved in creating any moment. I think of it simply as our part and God's part. On any given Sunday, I am only responsible to see that our team has—to the best of our ability—planned, created, and rehearsed for the possibility of moments that matter. Throughout the process, we get on our knees and ask our Father to empower, anoint, and move in human hearts as only he can. Analyzing the human dimension in no way denies how futile our efforts would be without the Holy Spirit's power and grace.

Our Part

Our part essentially involves selecting and crafting great raw material, designing the best flow for the service, and making room for attenders to respond to what they experience.

It All Starts with Great Material

In the previous chapter, we explored the absolute necessity of beginning with authentic people who communicate God's truth. Once we assemble a genuine team of Christ-followers, the focus moves to the quality of the material they deliver. Moments almost always begin with the selection or creation of great raw ingredients—music, drama scripts, video segments, etc. Initial decisions about songs or an approach to drama or video are enormously important—what we call *huge*! This is where it all starts. We frequently remind one another of the massive work involved in preparing any element we select. Every part of the service requires hours of writing, arranging, editing, and rehearsals. We must fiercely devote ourselves to choosing material that doesn't result in a so-what, ho-hum response.

We generate wise selection decisions by asking ourselves four questions about each potential element:

1. Does this piece move *us*?

2. Is it theologically sound and biblically true?

3. Does it have artistic integrity?

4. Is it tasteful?

1. Does this piece move us?

It's perfectly legitimate to begin by asking if team members themselves are moved by a song, drama idea, or video selection. After all, we've been entrusted with instincts, and we will be a part of the audience (even if we're not directly the target audience). When you play a song or read a script, watch how your brainstorming team reacts. Does everyone feel something? Can you describe to one another what you're feeling? If the prospective element generates little enthusiasm among team members, chances are good it will have the same result with the audience in the hour on Sunday—unless together you determine how to transform the material.

It's important to make selection decisions for all potential music and artistic elements together as a team. There is wisdom in a group and no one individual has perfect discernment.

Don't select material that fails to evoke passion from your own team. Wishful thinking will not transform that piece into something that has a radically different impact on Sunday morning attenders!

2. Is it theologically sound and biblically true?

Carefully review song lyrics to make sure they are theologically sound and consistent with Scripture. Unfortunately, over the years we have uncovered many songs that don't pass these tests, despite the fact that they were written by Christian artists. If in doubt, we ask our elders and teaching pastors to look over the lyrics and lend us their discernment. You must also scrutinize drama and video selections for theological and biblical truth.

3. Does it have artistic integrity?

Artistic integrity includes both the quality of the material and its correlation to real life. Ruthlessly avoid anything that comes across as preachy, simplistic, manipulative, or out of touch with authentic human experience. Some Christian artists write music or dramas that misrepresent life as always happy and without mystery or brokenness. If they do acknowledge pain and struggle, they are often quick to tie up everything with a fairy tale ending. Most of us recognize that life is not so simple, and those who show up on Sunday morning are not easily duped. The congregation quickly tunes out if they sense we are overly sweet and out of touch with life as they know it. The most effective art identifies with those in the audience, revealing truths about the human experience that are so personal and riveting, they cannot be denied.

First Man on the Moon, United States 10¢ stamp

MADE IN U.S.A. stamp

postmark: TUE NOV 4 1977

210

4. Is it tasteful?

Always remember that we are crafting church services, not concerts or theatrical productions. Creating art for Sunday morning includes working within the boundaries of good taste. Elements that might be acceptable for Christian artists to explore at another location on a Friday night may not pass the "but this is still church" test. For example, even if a character in a dramatic scene might believably curse in anger, we do not allow it on Sunday morning. We also pay close attention to humor that draws on the lowest common denominator, such as bathroom jokes or sexual innuendos. We aim for art at a higher level, art considered both truthful and tasteful. This sometimes requires excruciating decisions about scripts, video segments, and even dance choreography. Once again, there is wisdom in a team. We occasionally discern a need for the counsel of church leaders and pull them in for help when we get stuck.

Finding the Flow

Even if we've selected great material and crafted it with care, moments can elude us if we fail to create the best flow for the service. Sometimes I sit in the congregation eagerly anticipating an element I hope will move people, only to be disappointed. "Where did we go wrong?" our team asks. The individual pieces were strong, but we didn't weave them together quite right and the service never reached its potential.

Designing the flow of a service or event is an art in itself. Essentially, flow comes down to key decisions about the order of service, timing, and transitions.

Assembling the elements of any church service into the most effective order is like playing with the pieces of a puzzle until they fit just right. We don't have a service template with slots we try to fill every week. Even if your church follows a structured liturgy or a more traditional format, I still recommend paying careful attention to how each service element builds on the one before it.

We need to look at two kinds of flow—content flow and emotion/energy flow. Sometimes it seems logical that one element should follow another, but when we imagine it in advance we sense it won't feel right. If you're responsible for service planning, I urge you to sit down with a proposed service order on paper, and begin to imagine the way attenders might respond to each element. As much as possible, we try to avoid predictable patterns, so attenders won't go on autopilot.

Congregational worship can easily fall into ruts. Does every service begin with three high-energy worship choruses? Maybe at another church, every Sunday begins with one or two quiet hymns that then build to a crescendo with a majestic piece. Perhaps your team has established a service flow template that begins with drama and music, always followed by announcements. Review your service orders for the past few months. Do you see a high level of predictability? If so, consider whether it might be time to craft a new flow and see what God might do.

Once the team has agreed on a service order, the next essential step in crafting moments is timing and transitions. Timing centers on the tempo or rhythm of each individual element. I am continually amazed at how pacing for music, drama, or video affects a potential moment. Music at our church sometimes sounds like all the instrumentalists consumed way too much caffeine in rehearsal and are off to the races! On other Sundays, songs or theatrical pieces drag, lulling everyone into a yawn fest. Those who lead and direct these elements must hone their skills, learning to discern when timing is off and coaching teams to a more effective pace. It's hard to believe that minute tempo differences can impact the potential for a meaningful moment, but I have witnessed the contrast many times, especially as we change pacing from one service

CAFFEINE

NO caffeine

to the next. No lyrics or words are rewritten, and yet the entire piece feels so much better and has more power.

Transitions make a huge difference in creating an effective flow for the hour on Sunday. When our team fails to transition well from one element to the next, I'm reminded of learning to drive a stick shift Volkswagen. My going from one gear to the next without properly depressing the clutch created a jerky ride for my poor father and me! If we put together wonderful artistic pieces, yet fail to plan smooth transitions, the congregation will feel jerked around. They'll shift nervously as they wait for the next song to be counted off, or for the pastor to walk on the platform and assemble message notes, or for drama props to be removed during a clumsy silence.

Having learned the hard way through more than our fair share of awkward transitions, our team imagines in advance what will be required to move from one element to the next. We then talk it through with the keyboard player, stage team, and everyone else involved. Timing and transitions are inextricably linked. For example, if lights and music move too quickly out of a riveting drama, we risk diminishing the piece's power by propelling the audience on to something else before they are ready. On the other hand, we have sometimes held a light or left an actor in an uncomfortable position for too long.

Experiment to find just the right approach, and then rehearse delicate transitions until every team member gets in sync like a well-oiled machine. Sustain momentum by arranging the music flow that takes worshipers on a journey from one song to the next, rather than jerking them with starts and stops between every piece.

Making Room for Response

Once a team consistently selects great material and finds the right flow, the next level of maturity in crafting moments is making room for the congregation to respond. This is where our team has been most stretched in recent years. Although God enabled us to create some powerful pieces, we had not carefully explored how to help attenders process their experiences of these moments in church. Our pastor saw this weakness and called our team to experiment with what we now call

and the extension of moments.

Whether the Holy Spirit ambushes attenders through an artistic element or biblical teaching, we must provide opportunities for them to reflect on what is stirring in their souls. Before anyone heads to the parking lot, we want to give each one a chance to connect with God, to discern next steps, to move from being an observer to a true participant in the moment.

As one often entrusted to guide the congregation in spiritual direction, I have learned I must first enter personally into all the elements that lead up to moments. Everyone we ask to address the congregation following a moment gets preparation information well in advance. This includes lyrics and even CDs of the music, drama or video scripts and, ideally, an opportunity to watch the rehearsal so nothing is a surprise. The spiritual director for the congregation prays in advance for wisdom to read the room, and to be a conduit of what the Spirit seems to be doing in the moment. At times, this means guiding the congregation through a time of reflective prayer. It may mean crafting an exercise in which congregation members assess themselves on an issue and have an opportunity to write a response or dialog about it with someone sitting nearby. Sometimes a moment needs to be followed by silence. Silence provides a space for appropriate process, allowing attenders to live in the moment before moving on. It is vitally important to coach all those involved with the service to handle moments with care. Otherwise, we place ourselves at risk for encountering an enormous danger I call the violation of moments.

* SPIRITUAL DIRECTION

WE USE THE TERM SPIRITUAL DIRECTION TO DESCRIBE THIS CONGREGATIONAL PRACTICE WHILE RECOGNIZING THAT THE TERM IS MORE TRADITIONALLY USED TO DESCRIBE A ONE-ON-ONE PRACTICE OF PERSONAL GUIDANCE.

The Violation of Moments

Have you ever experienced a moment in church when a theatrical piece, song, or dance clearly touched nearly everyone in the room, almost took their breath away? And then, before you knew it, something or someone ruined that moment, yanked you and everyone else out of deep responses, and made you wonder if that person had any concept of what they just did. That's a violation of a moment.

The most common culprits are, unfortunately, pastors or others entrusted with moving on to announcements, the offering, or even the sermon. I have nightmares about this kind of thing. I imagine an incredibly powerful drama scene, music, or wor-

ship experience followed by a perky person bounding up on the platform to tell a joke, bombard everyone with announcements, or chat about the local sports team's prospects for that afternoon. Everything in me wants to scream, "Hello! Clue phone! Do you realize what you're doing?!!!" And yet moments are violated almost every Sunday in churches all over our planet. How can we prevent such tragic misses?

Protecting moments begins with viewing the hour on Sunday as one entire experience, not as individual slots, or as part one and part two. In some churches, an attender gets the impression that whatever precedes the sermon is pretty much a throwaway, a less-than element, merely a superficial appetizer to the substance that really counts—biblical teaching. I've actually witnessed Sunday mornings with pastors on the platform or in the front row during worship totally absorbed in their sermon notes and clearly ignoring what others on the platform are doing. Some pastors don't even show up until the service is well underway. What message does that send to the congregation?

We must look at our services as a unified experience that combines the arts with relevant teaching to create a carefully woven whole. We are ever so much stronger when we work together by allowing the arts to do what they do best and the teaching to accomplish what only biblical preaching can provide. This boils down to one thing—seeing ourselves as one team, passing a baton from one part to the next, and determining that together we possess greater potential to impact human lives. Therefore, each person who participates in front of the congregation—including the pastor and any other communicators—is best served by knowing in advance the entire plan for the service and the context that precedes and follows their roles.

On a practical level, such teamwork requires that every communicator be given all the tools required to understand each service element and its purpose. Our teaching pastors meet with the arts team on Wednesdays before weekend services to walk through the plan and identify potential moments in advance. When I am a part of the service, having this information enables me to withdraw and ask the Holy Spirit to help me discern how to respond to whatever moments I am asked to follow, and how to provide the congregation a bridge to what comes next. I enter the weekend with a plan, but also hold that plan loosely in case God moves in a different way than we had predicted.

Everyone who plays a part in the service must be *fully present and engaged.* It is essential for pastors to begin their part of the service with the appropriate tone, depending on what happened just before their walk to the pulpit. If we view ourselves as passing a baton from one part of the service to the next, we will all be far more intentional about receiving that baton smoothly and not

OOPS! REMOVE WEDDING IMAGES!!!

PSST!!!
Not that kind of engaged!

217

dropping it mid-race. We take tremendous care to craft services for potential moments—all the while recognizing that no true moment happens without God.

TEAcher

offering teAm

DRAMa Team

wOrsHip Team

God's Part

After a service, hundreds of men, women, and children lined up down three auditorium aisles, quietly waiting for a brief moment to stand on a narrow rock platform and pray with one of our pastors. That's a memory I will carry with me into old age. The moment began, as I believe all church moments do, with God whispering to our pastor and arts team. Part of a series titled *Life's Missing Ingredients*, that weekend service focused on security. While we recognized that many people in our community were feeling insecure in uncertain times, we completely underestimated their depth of need for Christ, our Solid Rock.

Early in the service, a drama depicted a husband in the middle of the night, frantically collecting household knives and scissors. His wife enters the kitchen and questions his odd behavior. She's been worried about her husband, who hasn't slept for three days and is deeply troubled. The attenders wonder, "What is wrong with this man?" Eventually we learn that the neighbor across the street, a father with three young children, recently committed suicide. That event disturbed this character profoundly, triggering guilt about his inability to prevent the tragedy and his failure to befriend the neighbor. Worse yet, the suicide aroused his own fears of coming unhinged. He thinks that collecting and hiding all his home's knives and scissors may perhaps protect his family and himself from any tragedy.

The wife attempts to speak sense into her husband, soothes his tears, and holds him. The scene ends with no great resolve, only with the wife convincing her distraught husband to leave the knife box for now and come to bed. After his exit, she stands alone by the kitchen table, tears flowing, unglued by the trauma that has invaded her once safe world.

During this scene, no one in the congregation moved, and they barely breathed. The lights slowly cross-faded to a vocalist on a stool, who began a tender song expressing our longings to feel safe and secure. The song was truly a lament for "a firm place to stand," and it turned our cries for strength and security toward God.

a team of artists developed a script

Before anyone could think to applaud, I took a deep breath, walked on the platform, and the lights cross-faded to me. All week I had prepared for the potential of this moment. I looked at the faces in front of me who identified, in varying degrees, with how wobbly our world often feels and how we

try to stuff down fears and anxiety. I asked people to identify what was making them feel shaky—family issues, economic worries, massive world turbulence, broken relationships. I guided them into prayer, encouraging them to bring to God the things keeping them awake at night and to ask God for peace. The end of the prayer slowly turned to a tone of trust and hope that led to a contemporary version of an old hymn, "Christ the Solid Rock." Gradually, a team of vocalists filled the platform, all pouring out their hearts as they expressed our need for Jesus to be that firm place to stand.

By the time our pastor came up to speak, the congregation was fully prepared for truth from the Bible. The majority had already admitted to themselves where they felt insecure and were longing for a description of how God can be trusted to help in this shaky world.

Just a few days prior, Bill had sensed where these moments might lead. He asked our production team to

then God moved a songwriter

Our pastor envisioned a prop

create a small space on stage for his message. It resembled a solid, rocky platform. He originally intended to use it as a visual prop. But the Holy Spirit had an even greater plan for that rock crafted by our artists. Bill's next prompting from God was to invite anyone who felt shaky to come up on the stage following the service and stand on that rock for a brief moment of prayer. He made clear that not everyone needed this, that many folks felt basically secure and could head home. But after our first service on that Saturday evening, he offered to stay and pray with anyone for whom it would be meaningful.

I hung down near the front of the stage and discerned after a few moments that Bill would need help. So many people lined up for prayer that he would never make it to the start of the next service if he did all the praying alone. I joined him on that tiny rock platform and put my arm on the shoulder of each individual who came to me for prayer. Standing on that symbolic rock was exceedingly significant for those who came forward. Some had tears in their eyes; others simply bowed their heads and

received a touch and words of prayer on their behalf. In subsequent services, we recruited more church leaders to help with all those who wanted to pray. Late Saturday night, our production team created a much wider rock-like platform, knowing that on Sunday morning there would be even larger crowds and we would never all fit on the original space. After the final Sunday service, with at least a dozen people leading prayers, the lines still extended out into the lobby. We prayed for over an hour with folks. What a moment for our church! At the end of that Sunday, we all knew that something truly

an experience of prayer

supernatural had taken place, and we stood in awe at the power of our almighty God.

The Holy Spirit's part in all the moments of that service trace back to a month before, when a team of artists first developed a script about knives in a kitchen. Then God moved a songwriter to respond to that piece, and he wrote the lament, "A Firm Place to Stand." The Spirit led me in a time of solitude at a coffee shop, trying to prepare for how to follow that moment. And then the most pivotal leadings of all came when our pastor envisioned a prop, and he followed a prompting to offer an experience of prayer that literally thousands of people clearly needed. The supernatural dimension of all the moments in that service was evident from beginning to end. We did our part—responding, crafting, and praying individually and as a team for God's anointing. And then God showed up again and again, from brainstorming all the way to the service itself. God did what only he can do—he touched human hearts.

When all is said and done, I believe we all long to be part of creating and experiencing tran-

God touched human hearts

scendent moments. And the wonder of it all is that God chooses to partner with people like me and like you to advance his kingdom on this earth. I believe the potential for moments that matter exists in every church, as we listen for God's guidance, develop our crafts, and pray like crazy for supernatural power to be unleashed. Instead of attenders simply thinking about their plans for Sunday afternoon, they can start up their cars admitting, "I was moved." What an incredible privilege we have to play a part in the business of life transformation.

It never gets old.

Questions to Explore

1. Recall a moment when you were personally moved in church. What contributed to that experience touching you so deeply?

2. When selecting material for your Sunday services, which of the four questions does your team need to pay more attention to? (Does this piece move us? Is it theologically sound and biblically true? Does it have artistic integrity? Is it tasteful?) How can you improve your selection process?

3. Describe the most typical order of service for your hour on Sunday. Has this flow become predictable? What alternative steps can you experiment with?

4. Assess your team's attention to timing and transitions. What might you do to improve the quality of both?

5. In what ways is there room in your services for the congregation to respond? Brainstorm options for allowing space for your attenders to process their experiences.

6. Can you recall a time when a moment was violated in your church? How prepared is each communicator for the context of their role in the service? In what ways can the baton be passed more smoothly from one part of the service to the next?

7. Evaluate the part prayer plays in your entire process. In what specific ways can your team more consistently access the power of prayer from brainstorming all the way through to the hours on Sunday?

chapter twelve

When
Scripture
is skillfully
communicated,
people far
from God
are drawn
to know him,
and believers
are built
up in the
faith.

"I'd like you to give the message on Mother's Day weekend," my pastor calmly stated in a one-on-one meeting several years ago.

"Exc me?

use "

I stammered.

His request immediately catapulted me from the artist chair to the teacher hot seat. I was propelled into another world entirely—from a place where I was a casual analyst of countless sermons and teachers to being the teacher myself. This new world terrified me. Up until then, I had spoken to our congregation in brief segments only—reading Scripture, delivering comments, communicating information. Teaching a thirty- to forty-minute message was way beyond my comfort zone. On top of that, I had only been a mother for four years. I certainly didn't consider myself a parenting expert. What could I possibly say to thousands of people about motherhood?

In a moment of weakness, I said yes, ushering in a month of tremendous anxiety and hard work. I began to study and write. I asked for help from my pastor and other teachers I deeply respected. I read the entire message to my husband, my pastor, and anyone else who would give me feedback. And then the moment arrived when I walked up to the lectern, set down my notes, and took a deep breath. With shaky knees—literally—and a tentative voice, I spoke the first words of my first sermon. That experience was an odd mixture of fear, growth, and even exhilaration. God used me to encourage other moms, and I drove away from the church that day filled with a sense of wonder at the thrill of being a messenger of truth.

The process of preparing and delivering that message began a journey of bridging two worlds—the world of church artists and the world of teaching pastors. It's a journey  that continues to this day. God provided me a window into both worlds, giving me a deeper understanding of the challenges and potential of each vital part of the hour on Sunday. I discovered that after listening to sermons my entire life, I actually knew more than I thought I did about crafting a message. In the process, I also learned that teaching is one of my gifts, a gift I had not allowed to flourish, partly because of my gender (having no female role models to follow) and partly because of my leadership focus on the arts. And like the wise saying goes, only by "walking in someone else's shoes" can we fully understand what it's like to steward their gift and responsibilities. Today I have a lot more empathy for teachers!

More than ever before, I long for people who attend church to drive away saying, "That message impacted me." Transformational teaching is the foundation of any powerful hour on Sunday.

MENU

The Main Course

If we think of the hour on Sunday as a painstakingly and lovingly prepared gourmet meal, the teaching portion of the meal could be described as the main course.

$22.00 per person

Side Dishes

Even if the appetizers, the side dishes, and the dessert (my personal favorite) are all to die for, a weak main course leaves the diner disappointed with the entire meal.

$4.95 additional

Soups

Similarly, those attending church can experience a powerful expression of the arts, including a transcendent moment, and yet leave feeling frustrated if the sermon is mediocre. They will head to the parking lot thinking it was a bad day in church. And if the sermon is strong, a less-than-stellar arts portion probably will not ruin the gourmet meal.

$4.95 cup $6.95 bowl

Dessert

After ten chapters exploring the potential of the arts, the reader may be shocked by my point of view, but I think it's true—teaching matters most. Thankfully, however, we're not in a contest, and the best hours on Sunday skillfully weave the arts and biblical teaching into a dynamic experience, a superb meal from start to finish.

$7.95 plain $8.95 a la mode

All services accompanied by arts and biblical teaching.
Sunday services subject to change without notice.

Why is transformational teaching so essential to the vitality of every local church? Acts 2:42 states that the first Christians "devoted themselves to the apostles' teaching." When Scripture is skillfully communicated, people far from God are drawn to know him, and believers are built up in the faith. It is the primary way we are equipped for service, for becoming increasingly more like Jesus, for living out what we say we believe.

Teaching also ignites every biblical value a local church stands for. Without strong teaching, it is exceedingly difficult to call people to care for their lost friends, serve God with their gifts, live in loving community with other believers, give generously to God's work, or resolve conflicts according to scriptural guidelines. Show me a church that consistently and compellingly receives and acts on teaching about these core values, and I'll show you a healthy church.

There are some who contend that perhaps teaching's vital role is receding. Today some churches devote the majority of their attention to worship or experiential interaction rather than to teaching. I believe this is a serious error. While we always need to discern cultural trends, there will forever be a need for teaching that God uses to transform lives. We should focus on crafting teaching that has the greatest potential to make a difference.

People far wiser and more experienced than I have written numerous resources to help teachers hone and improve their skills. I simply want to highlight key ingredients of great messages and then consider how artists and teachers can more effectively work together. ✱

Ingredients of a Great Message

During leadership meetings, one of my coworkers occasionally pulls a stuffed animal from his bookshelf and plants it on the conference table. It's an elephant. The elephant indicates that there's something no one wants to acknowledge or face, an issue that is silently impacting our decisions and should not be ignored. It's the proverbial elephant in the room.

✱ I AM INDEBTED TO BILL HYBELS AND JOHN ORTBERG FOR MANY OF THE INSIGHTS THAT FOLLOW.

There are elephants in churches everywhere. Through whispered conversations with music directors, worship leaders, and artists from churches all over the world, I've learned about an elephant that commonly lurks around the table of their church meetings. The elephant is this: the person who most frequently delivers the message on Sunday mornings does not have a teaching gift. He or she may be an effective pastor, shepherd, or administrator. But when that pastor goes up to the pulpit on Sunday mornings, the majority of listeners brace themselves to endure another meandering, mediocre sermon. This should not be so! The primary ingredient of a great message is that it is delivered by a person who has a teaching gift.

I am deeply grateful that our elders have fiercely protected the pulpit at Willow Creek, allowing only those who have teaching gifts to bring the message. Potential teachers are given opportunities in smaller settings or sub ministries so others can ascertain over time if, indeed, God has given them a teaching gift. All teachers can improve their skills, but before we choose to subject our congregation to a budding teacher's words, we need to have confidence that they possess the basic gift. I long for every congregation to be protected in just this way.

So what are a church and its key leaders to do if it's clear that the pastor does not have strong enough teaching gifts? I only know that courageous, difficult, and sensitive conversations—with appropriate process—are required to bring out the truth in love and seek God-honoring solutions. For the sake of our congregations and people we long to reach in our community, this elephant must not be ignored.

Okay. I got that off my chest.

Now, assuming we have teachers teaching, let's explore the ingredients of a great message. I believe transformational teaching is biblical, passionate, relevant, creative, and honest.

Biblical

Our first of ten values at Willow Creek states, "We believe that anointed teaching is the catalyst for transformation in individuals' lives and in the church."

We view every *message given at* our church through the lens of faithfulness *to biblical truth,* and, equally important, its application *of that truth to* human lives.

What qualifies a message as biblical? We are not referring to the style of a message. Some Christians believe a message isn't truly biblical unless it's taught in an expository, verse-by-verse style with numerous references to the original language. Our measurement of whether a message is biblical transcends style. Instead, it focuses on whether the teaching is inspired and supported by Scripture and whether it leads listeners to wrestle with how these truths will matter to them Monday through Saturday. Our elders challenge any teaching that diminishes the Bible's core truths and doctrines.

It is vital that our congregations, over time, are taught from a variety of biblical passages and themes. Otherwise we run the risk that teachers will choose only those subjects and parts of Scripture that most appeal to them personally, and our congregations will not receive a balanced diet. Teaching is not fundamentally about information delivery. Accumulating biblical knowledge does not necessarily result in meaningful life change. For that to take place, other ingredients must come into play.

Passionate

My daughters attend a summer camp for thirteen days every year. As part of the closing ceremonies, the campers head off to an activity so the camp director can speak to the parents. The director uses stories and biblical truth to drill home his fundamental message that our world's future depends on healthy families, that our homes launch young people into lives that make a difference. Every year he tells the same corny stories, and every year his eyes fill with tears. But his message gets me every time. I walk away inspired to be more committed to my husband and daughters, to give them more of myself, and to lean into God's strength and wisdom as a wife and mother. The camp director's urgency is the key. I love his passion.

Every time a teacher takes a deep breath and begins to speak, listeners wonder how much that teacher really cares about the subject matter. Within a few moments, we are either drawn in or we begin to yawn, because the speaker doesn't seem all that excited. Passion doesn't come out of every speaker in just the same way. But we recognize its presence (or lack) no matter what. Are we being called to greater levels of servant-hood? Then we should sense the teacher—at least for this Sunday—believes nothing matters more. If the subject matter is humility, then, for right now, that's the supreme character trait the teacher most aspires to.

Teachers become passionate as a result of intentional study, personal discoveries of biblical truth, and living with their message material all week long. (For some teachers, it's a week; for me—the slowest message writer I know—it's more like a month!) Most teachers can't help but look at all of life through the grid of whatever their next message is about. We search for evidence of its importance while we hunt for illustrations. By the time we get up to speak on Sunday morning, we are genuinely convinced of the essential truths God has given us to communicate. Passion can't help but spill over. Our sense of urgency is intimately connected with another key ingredient—relevance.

Relevant

Bill Hybels and John Ortberg have three primary questions they ask me and other teachers whenever we're preparing a message:

1. What do you want people to know?

2. What do you want people to feel?

3. WHAT DO YOU WANT PEOPLE TO DO?

At the end of the day, the purpose of teaching is changed lives. My goal as a teacher should go beyond making people more biblically literate. Unless listeners are becoming more and more like Jesus Christ—more loving, kind, patient, generous, humble, peaceful, and joyful—our teaching is truly a waste of time. The prophet Ezekiel described the tragedy of messages that fail to transform:

EZEKIEL 33

[31]My people come to you, as they usually do, and sit before you to listen to your words, but they do not put them into practice. With their mouths they express devotion, but their hearts are greedy for unjust gain. [32]Indeed, to them you are nothing more than one who sings love songs with a beautiful voice and plays an instrument well, for they hear your words but do not put them into practice.

PROPS

I never want attenders to head home muttering, "So what?" In the process of preparing a message, teachers must ruthlessly ask themselves how people will be any different after listening to and applying what is taught. If we can't answer these questions, we must begin again, no matter how enamored we may be with our brilliant insights.

I grew up listening to many sermons that were simply unclear. I didn't understand their take-home value. While some folks may have been impressed with the teacher's biblical knowledge, I wondered what to do with the seemingly unrelated pieces of information. Perhaps those experiences served me well. I am fiercely devoted to crafting relevant messages, asking God to show me what he wants his children to hear, understand, and do as a result of the teaching. Knowing how little any of us ultimately retains of what we hear, I strive to discern the essential and specific life change I long to see in listeners' lives.

Creative

What grabbed me first was the huge, shiny motorcycle. Various modes of transportation lined our church platform, from a baby walker on one end to a walker for elderly people on the other. Our guest speaker delivered a message titled "From Walker to Walker," based on the psalm that urges us to treasure our days, to seize life, knowing how brief our time on earth will be. The teacher's masterful use of props and stories brought to life biblical truth that enabled listeners to remember and apply the teaching long after we headed home.

More than ever, those who teach must embrace the value of creativity. Why more than ever? Two reasons: because we increasingly communicate to a culture overwhelmed by information; and we communicate to generations who learn as much by seeing and experiencing as they do by listening. Most listeners' attention spans are dwindling. Words simply aren't enough, much of the time.

In the past few years, Willow Creek teachers have increased their use of props, images, and words on a screen, stories, or congregational experiences in messages. It's rare to hear a message without such elements.

We've had a potter up front crafting a vase during an entire message about God's instructions for us to be "good clay." We've passed out tiny mustard seeds to bring to life the scripture about how powerful even a small amount of faith can be. I've witnessed science experiments, drama sketches in the middle of a sermon, video clips to illustrate a point, and a teacher whacking open a whole watermelon as he taught about integrity. While some may label such methods as frivolous entertainment, I counter that the creativity resulted in teaching that the average person could remember and relate to everyday life.

It reminds me of the style of Jesus, the greatest teacher of all. Jesus Christ was unlike any Jewish leader who taught in the synagogues. Jesus pointed to a fig tree, a withered hand, and a praying widow to make his points. He was a master storyteller, regaling his listeners with tales of farmers, shepherds, and a rich man preparing a great banquet. Whatever was most familiar, most personal, easiest to grasp and apply—Jesus used it to illustrate truth. No teacher since has been more creative or more compelling.

As a teacher, I face the same blank sheet artists face. When I wrestle with the biblical truth God has called me to proclaim, I ask the same questions: How can I bring this to life? What will help the congregation understand God's Word and then discern what difference it should make after the hour on Sunday? Until a teacher has determined the answer to these questions, he or she has only partially prepared. I am learning to study first, to fill my mind with God's truth, with historical and cultural understanding as I interpret the Bible, and then—equally important—to move to a creative phase where I do not quit until I receive the aha moment that comes when I know how to communicate the message creatively.

During a recent holiday season, between Thanksgiving and Christmas, I was asked to teach a message about extended family relationships. We know many people struggle during the holidays. We hope our family gatherings will look and feel like warm-hearted Norman Rockwell paintings. Rarely do they reach our expectations! I studied biblical passages concerning how we should relate to one another and read books by family experts. Sometime during that process, I received my aha moment.

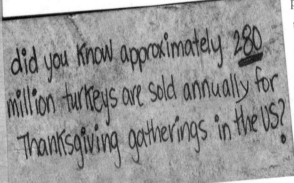
did you know approximately 280 million turkeys are sold annually for Thanksgiving gatherings in the US?

I pictured a table on our church platform, set with beautiful china, place cards, and a lovely centerpiece. There needed to be at least eight chairs at the table, representing an extended family gathering. Throughout the message, I would use items familiar to everyone as symbols of how we need to relate. The place cards, saltshaker, water

glasses, and knives all became my teaching tools. I would walk over to the table, pick up an item, and proceed to teach and apply. When listeners experienced their own family gatherings, they could look at the table, see those same items, and hopefully remember the truths from Sunday morning. I was deeply grateful to the Holy Spirit for an idea that brought that message to life. **It was time for a happy dance!** I believe that more than ever, creativity counts. One final trait of effective teaching matters every bit as much.

Honest

The final ingredient of a great message is honesty. In the chapter on authenticity we explored how essential it is for the hour on Sunday to be truthful about the human condition. This honesty is as significant for the teaching as it is for the arts portion of our services. Listeners desperately need teaching pastors to speak the truth. We long to trust that the person behind the pulpit lives in the same challenging world we live in, understands our struggles, and refuses to deliver mere platitudes or simplistic formulas to address complex issues and thorny problems.

A huge part of honesty in messages comes from personal illustrations told in appropriate ways. This doesn't mean the teacher should tell the congregation every personal sin, family story, or intimate moment. But appropriate self-disclosure is a tool that effectively establishes a strong connection with listeners. Such disclosures build bridges that probably can't be built in any other way. The congregation recognizes that the teacher knows what it's like to face challenges in the family, workplace, neighborhood, finances, and culture. The teacher is perceived either as one of us or as totally other—a religious figure unmarred by everyday living.

Frederick Buechner is a writer and preacher who knows what it is to face a congregation and deliver a sermon. In his classic book *Telling the Truth*, Buechner offers this wisdom to teachers of God's Word:

But let him take heart.
He is called not to be an actor,
a magician,
in the pulpit.

He is called to be himself. He is
called to tell the truth as he has experienced it. He is called to be human,
to be human, and that is calling
enough for any man. If he does not
make real to them the human experience of what it is to cry into the
storm and receive no answer, to be
sick at heart and find no healing, then
he becomes the only one there who
seems not to have had that experience because most surely under their
bonnets and shawls and jackets,
under their afros and pony-tails, all
the others have had it whether they
talk of it or not. As much as anything
else, it is their experience of the
absence of God that has brought
them there in search of his presence,
and if the preacher does not speak of
that and to that, then he becomes like
the captain of a ship who is the only
one aboard who either does not know
that the waves are

twenty feet high

and the decks awash or will not face
up to it so that anything else he tries
to say by way of hope and comfort
and empowering becomes suspect on
the basis of that one crucial igno-
rance or disingenuousness or cow-
ardice or reluctance to speak in love
any truths but the ones that people
love to hear.

Those of us entrusted with the responsibility to teach must resist the temptation to make life sound easier than it really is. God will show us how to bring hope and healing without being dishonest.

What a holy calling teachers have! To be biblical, passionate, relevant, creative, and honest is a tall order. No wonder Paul earnestly warned Timothy to never neglect his teaching gift: "Be diligent in these matters; give yourself wholly to them, so that everyone may see your progress. Watch your life and doctrine closely. Persevere in them, because if you do, you will save both yourself and your hearers" (1 Timothy 4:15–16).

Teachers and Artists Working Together

There is a wall in some churches. It's not a brick-and-mortar wall, but it's a wall nonetheless. Though the barrier is not usually talked about, its presence hurts the hour on Sunday more than we know. This wall divides the artists preparing one part of the service from the teacher who will deliver the message. In most cases, the wall was not erected out of malice or intolerance, yet it effectively blocks communication. What contributes most to this wall is the overwhelmingly rapid pace of ministry combined with a lack of vision for what services could be if the wall were torn down. Then teachers and artists might actually work closely together, crafting whole experiences for their congregations instead of part one and part two.

In recent years at Willow, I've seen the wall between teachers and artists almost entirely obliterated. More than ever before, our teachers and artists are collaborating, passing batons back and forth to one another in the creation of powerful hours on Sunday.

Obliterating the wall requires sacrifices. It requires more time

BRICK WALL

GOING... GOING...

GONE!!!

from both the teachers and the artists—and time is truly our most precious commodity. Some arts teams tell me they must beg every week, through e-mails, voice mail, and every other means to eke out morsels of information from their pastors about upcoming message topics and themes. Information is helpful.

Interaction is ever so much better. Despite their huge responsibilities, our teachers recognize the value of meeting regularly with the arts team to plan weekend services. Every week they gather on Wednesday to go over the plan for the upcoming Sunday as well as kick around ideas and concepts for future services. Often a song or drama idea ignites a teacher to take the message in a new direction. Our teachers have grown creatively by exchanging ideas with the artists. Frequent interaction also helps avoid major surprises and prevents the dreaded violation of moments. We see ourselves more and more as a team, with mutual respect for each part. We haven't always worked so effectively together, so we treasure this new day and celebrate how we better serve the people who trust us to craft a meaningful hour on Sunday.

Navigating in harmony with artists and teachers is never easy. We still have our share of conflicts, misunderstandings, and what we call ouches. I am frequently contacted by pastors frustrated with their arts teams and artists who long for a stronger connection and support from their pastors. Let's not underestimate the challenge of working well together. Based on what I hear from our own team, along with input from church leaders around the world,

i've assembled a brief list of what teachers and artists wish their counterparts better understood about their work and challenges.

WISH-THEY-UNDERSTOOD LIST

by Nancy Beach

WHAT **PASTORS/TEACHERS**

WISH ARTISTS UNDERSTOOD ABOUT...

MESSAGE INFORMATION

My scope of responsibility is huge. I have far more to focus on than just meeting with you and giving you message information. I am doing the best I can.

FEEDBACK

I respond to loving, constructive requests, evaluation and dialog—I don't want to feel attacked or slandered. Tone of voice is very important to me. I do not want to feel like I'm walking on eggshells in every meeting with the artistic team. I need to be able to give constructive criticism without fear of someone's defensiveness or emotional fragility. I need to know we are all big people, with the church's best interests on the top of our priority list.

CHANGES

I sincerely want my teaching to be Spirit-led. There are times I need to make changes in what I have communicated to you for the sake of the church. I will try to make these rare exceptions.

WORKLOAD

I need you to recognize that I have huge leadership responsibilities that require my attention, and I can't give the totality of my time to crafting messages and interacting with artists.

MY JOB

What I do is really hard.

MESSAGE INFORMATION

We want to serve the church with the best possible material. We can't do our job without advance notice (not two days before Sunday!).

FEEDBACK

We long to have your feedback— good and bad. Please give your constructive criticism in the context of support and affirmation. We need to know you are for us and not live in fear of your criticism. And we love to work together, seeing you build parts of your message based on what we've created.

CHANGES

Our process involves many steps, rehearsals, and several people. Changes are more complicated than you know.

WORKLOAD

We have real limits in our capacity for creative output. We can't keep delivering great material without reasonable breaks. We desperately need your support for the resources required to build depth on our teams and to occasionally bring in guests to help out.

OUR JOB

What we do is really hard.

One Sunday in February

If teaching is ultimately about transformation, then any teacher longs to know that genuine life change occurs because of the hour on Sunday. We live for those times when God anoints the artists and the message to clearly move in the lives of real people. I had an incredible experience of witnessing the power of transformation on a cold Sunday in February. My assignment was a new one for me. Until that weekend, I had never taught a sermon designed to present the gospel message, painting a picture of what it truly means to be a Christian, and then inviting a response. Talk about an intimidating assignment for any teacher! I knew for certain that eternities were on the line, and I prepared like crazy to do my part.

As I prepared, the Holy Spirit brought to mind the image of a pyramid. I saw the names of God's traits (such as Redeemer, Father, and Shepherd)—key dimensions of how we learn to relate to him—as ascending in the form of a pyramid. Using lightweight building materials, our visual artists crafted blocks illustrating each trait. As I taught, they assembled these blocks behind me, eventually using a ladder to place the final pieces. I gave the message in parts, with drama and music elements illustrating dimensions of our relationship with God.

I was filled with passion as I described God as best I could—what could give any Christ-follower a greater sense of urgency? With other staff pastors, I'd carefully talked through options for closing the message. I knew the final moments would be critical. I needed to be clear and to invite listeners to pray with me if they were ready to receive Christ as Savior, Leader, and Friend. The staff and I prayed all week that God would do a mighty work that Sunday.

Nothing could have prepared me for the wonder of that final moment, that call to cross the line of faith. I asked everyone to bow their heads, and then explained one last time what it means to follow Jesus. I guided those who were ready through a prayer. Then I gave them the option—with the rest of the people still bowing their heads—to look up and briefly raise their hand to me, signaling their decision and sealing it in that moment. I looked up, wondering if any would be so bold to raise their hand, if God had brought anyone to this crossroad.

I WAS STUNNED.

Hand after hand went up all over the auditorium. For a second, I wondered if I had said it right, or if they were confused. But I knew this was the real deal. These people meant business. They would be in heaven with me forever because of that day. I was so choked up with gratitude and awe I could barely lead the final prayer. Since then, some of those folks have cited that February Sunday as they've been baptized in our lake. Nothing can possibly compare to the fulfillment of being an agent of transformation, one who proclaims the best news of all to a lost and searching generation. Teachers are blessed with that privilege and entrusted with that responsibility.

WHAT A GIFT.

Questions to Explore

1. How highly does your church uphold the value of teaching? Consider those who regularly teach. Is there an "elephant in the room" concerning whether any of them truly has a teaching gift? If so, what steps can be taken to have the right conversations or to help the pastor improve in his or her teaching?

2. As you look at the five ingredients of a great message—biblical, passionate, relevant, creative, honest—which one(s) are strongest at your church? Which need greater emphasis?

3. Recall a recent Sunday morning message. How would you rate that sermon (from 1 to 10) on relevance? What would you say the teacher wanted people to think, feel, and do differently when they left church?

4. Look over the two lists about pastors/teachers and artists. Which issues ring most true to you in terms of your need to more clearly understand those in the other camp? Describe specific ways you believe teachers and artists at your church could work together more effectively to craft the hour on Sunday.

chapter **thirteen**

If the
almighty
Creator
has
called
you to
serve the
church
with artistic
or teaching
gifts,
you have
the very
highest
of callings.

My original dream was to be a Hollywood producer. I believed God was calling me to the West Coast to immerse myself in a culture where I might make an impact by creating films and television programs reflecting a Christian worldview. I pursued an education to prepare for that dream, but in my mid-twenties, God redirected my path. He called me to a local church. The word *calling* may sound mysterious and perhaps even a little grandiose. I only know that one summer, after an intense period of prayer, fasting, and wrestling with God, I recognized that my Creator was leading me to pursue a different dream—to build a community of artists who would collaborate to create moments of transcendence in church. My Hollywood dream would need to be lived out by others.

I doubt anyone reading this book would say that unleashing the arts in a church setting is an easy path. It certainly won't lead to fame and fortune. Most of us have known times of intense discouragement, serious self-doubt, financial struggle, relational breakdowns, and creative burnout. We face blank sheets of paper and our share of critics every week. Those who volunteer their artistic gifts in church do so after long days in the marketplace or full-time homemaking. In addition to lengthy weeknight rehearsals, much of their precious weekend time is sacrificed to participate in services. More than once (okay, a lot more), I admit I've thought about quitting, and occasionally I've even allowed myself to fantasize about that original dream, wondering if following the path to Hollywood would have yielded a more fulfilling return.

And then I had lunch with Leo. He and his wife, Joy, were new to our church and asked to meet with me. Leo is a Christian about my age who has lived out my childhood dream in a way, as a writer and producer of major films and television series. After several years working on the West Coast and establishing his career, Leo and his family moved to the Chicago area, where they have roots. He now commutes to Los Angeles whenever necessary for his work. Our first lunch together was absolutely delightful. We exchanged stories about work and life, and I learned how Leo attempts to live out his faith through his profession. He said his

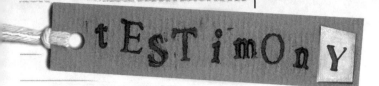
During a particulary bad period four years ago, friends brought us to see the play *Jairus*. It was the first time I heard a religious message I understood and the first time I ever cried in a house of worship— what a feeling! Since that time we have attended services regularly and in February I accepted Jesus Christ as my Lord and Savior.

Al Barron

victories have been few, but he tries to live a life of integrity in that world.

Leo asked for the meeting to explore how he might contribute his gifts at our church. We kicked around possibilities and, in connections since then, are working toward a creative contribution he can make through his writing and expertise. I'm excited about what might happen.

But here's the main reason I tell this story. God had a message for me as I drove back to church from that first lunch with Leo. I didn't hear an audible voice, but this is what I sensed the Lord impressing upon me in my little Camry: "Nance, Leo is living the life you thought you wanted. I called him to that. But let's play this out. What if you had pursued a producing role in L.A. and even had a measure of success? One day, as a Christ-follower, you would knock on the door of an arts leader at a local church, wherever you lived. You'd be asking that person to lunch and hoping to find some way—any way—you might use your gifts to make a direct difference in people's lives through Sunday services. You'd be longing for tangible evidence that what you create has an impact for eternity."

That moment jolted me. I'm thrilled God calls some of his followers like Leo to Hollywood, Broadway, and Nashville—we need believers in those arenas. But my Creator gently reminded me of the wonders I've experienced so far on the canvas of my one and only life. I had no idea what the rewards of this path to the church would be. How could I have foreseen the glorious results of transformed lives, artists joining the adventure, and deep personal fulfillment? Such are the rewards awaiting all who take this path.

Transformed Lives

One by one they cautiously stepped up to a microphone in the aisles of our church. Moments before being baptized, each stated his or her name and briefly thanked individuals who helped bring them to Christ. Because the arts team was so immersed in making sure the service went smoothly, we didn't have a chance to really listen to the stories until we viewed the video later. Face after face appeared on the screen. Several folks mentioned a specific Sunday service that helped them make a decision for Christ. Most spoke with tremendous emotion and gratitude for family, friends, and our church. Young people thanked their parents, twenty-somethings spoke of returning to God, and elderly folks described arduous life journeys God had redeemed.

After just ten minutes of watching that powerful video, our team was overwhelmed

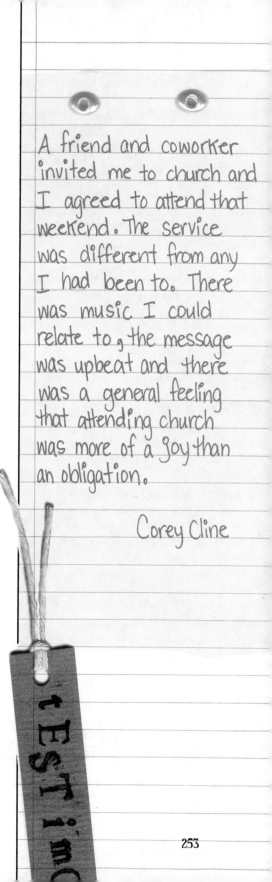

A friend and coworker invited me to church and I agreed to attend that weekend. The service was different from any I had been to. There was music I could relate to, the message was upbeat and there was a general feeling that attending church was more of a joy than an obligation.

Corey Cline

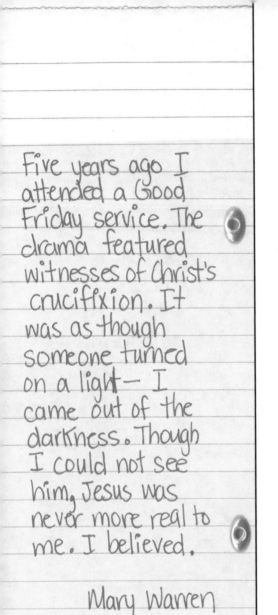

Five years ago I attended a Good Friday service. The drama featured witnesses of Christ's crucifixion. It was as though someone turned on a light— I came out of the darkness. Though I could not see him, Jesus was never more real to me. I believed.

Mary Warren

with emotion. The people we saw on screen will be in heaven one day, and God gave us the privilege of helping them on their spiritual journeys. We were more than ready to sign up for another ministry season!

Take a moment to mentally scroll through names and faces of people in your church. Think of someone who has come to faith through your community. Now call to mind a few more people—someone who discovered spiritual gifts, someone else who found healing for family relationships, another who learned how to manage money, care for her body, or worship his Creator in new ways. Can you think of specific names? Those *people*, those eternal souls, are the fruit of your labor. And *people* are what matter most to God.

Whether your Sunday services sowed or watered the seeds, God used you and your team to impact people in ways that count for eternity. Nothing matters more. If your contribution is playing an instrument, running the sound board, setting up the stage, writing scripts, leading worship, arranging music, aiming lights, acting in a drama, or delivering the message—

tESTimOnY

you contributed to the advancement of God's kingdom on planet Earth. Every ministry is a scrapbook of faces, with new pages added every year. As we turn the pages of the scrapbook and look at each person's eyes, we're reminded of his or her story, of the impact of our church on that individual's one and only life. *Life change.* There's nothing more rewarding.

Artists Joining the Adventure

There's another section in your scrapbook and mine, one that includes portraits of the staff and volunteer artists who have discovered the joy and fulfillment of using their gifts for God's purposes. Allow me to briefly tell the stories of a few of our faithful artists at Willow, trusting that their journeys closely mirror servants from your church as well. These stories represent a big part of why it's worth it to invest our lives in the arts ministry of a local church.

As you read each story, I suspect a face from your own ministry scrapbook might come to mind.

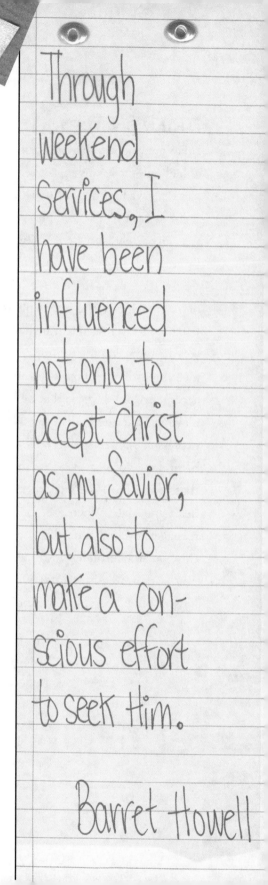

Through weekend services, I have been influenced not only to accept Christ as my Savior, but also to make a conscious effort to seek Him.

Barret Howell

BRIAN'S STORY

Brian grew up in suburban Chicago listening to southern gospel music. He was captivated by the bass guitar, and his parents gave him one as an eighth-grade graduation present. Self-taught, Brian started playing with the student ministry that ultimately launched Willow Creek. Thirty years later, Brian is still part of our music ministry!

By profession, Brian is a bricklayer. He is also the father of five children. He is quiet and unassuming, with a great laugh and a warm smile. Life hasn't been easy for Brian. One year he dropped out of ministry during a painful divorce. After meeting with one of our worship leaders, Brian felt so much acceptance and support that he eventually agreed to return to playing. Brian is a man of few words; he feels uncomfortable expressing himself verbally. He says, "When I play the bass behind our vocalists, I feel as though I'm communicating truth, that I assist in the delivery of a message I believe with all my heart and soul." When I see Brian play, I still view him as a teenager, a young man who discovered the part he could play early on and faithfully contributes week after week, year after year, with a sweet spirit and quiet strength. I sure can't quit as long as Brian keeps on inspiring me!

cOmmunicAtinG Truth

RHONDA'S STORY

No one in Rhonda's family was a dancer. The piano lessons her mother encouraged bored Rhonda and she begged to study dance instead. Her dream was to join a professional dance company. Pursuing that passion led Rhonda to the highest levels of dance in New York City and Chicago, culminating in a four-year run with the premier troupe of her dreams—the Hubbard Street Dance Company. She achieved her goal and traveled to Europe and throughout North America, soaring with that outstanding group.

However, something troubled Ronda. She loved Jesus Christ—had known him for most of her life—and was starving to serve him in some way. One day as she expressed this longing in a phone call with a fellow dancer, her phone clicked signaling another call. The caller was a friend asking Rhonda if she'd ever heard of a church called Willow Creek. "As a matter of fact," Rhonda replied, "I've started attending there." The friend asked Rhonda if she'd be willing to dance for the upcoming Easter services at the church. Would she ever! Rhonda knew this could not be a coincidence, but definitely a *God thing*. She literally jumped in with both feet.

Between services on that Easter weekend, I saw Rhonda in the tunnel area below the stage, stretching her muscles and preparing to use her body to express grief at the foot of the cross and then joy at the empty tomb. Rhonda was glowing. Her eyes filled with tears as she described the wonder of using her gift for God's purposes. Rhonda continued to dance with Hubbard Street for the next couple years, but her fulfillment there began to pale in comparison to the passion she felt for ministry.

These days, Rhonda has a new dream. She is working to establish a dance company at our church that is as excellent as Hubbard Street, but with an entirely different mission—to serve Christ. Her dream is well on its way to reality, delighting all of us who watch her progress and celebrate what only dance can bring to our congregation.

CHAR'S STORY

Char found our church during tremendous pain in her life. Born in Jamaica, she came from a strict religious background and had sung in church as a young girl. Music provided a refuge for Char when her parents divorced, and, though she was a quiet child, singing brought her out and gave her life. She eventually moved to Pittsburgh, married, and started a family. The darkest time of Char's life was an inexplicable depression that lasted about two years. She was the mother of two young girls, the wife of a music minister, and a leader in her church. Talking to God and writing music provided her only relief from depression. Char poured out her heart through crafting songs and, eventually, began to sense her sadness lifting.

After moving to Chicago for a recording opportunity with a company that eventually went bust, Char and her husband were once again at a low point and without a church home. They drove by Willow Creek one day and decided to give it a try the very next Sunday. Char describes her experience at Willow as one of God bringing healing. She and her husband wept through many services and felt they had found a new home where they could worship and grow. After many months, Char stepped out of the shadows to explore the music ministry, tentatively wondering if she could ever sing at Willow.

Char is an answer to prayer on many levels. First and foremost, her family is getting healthy, and her daughters' resentment against church is waning as they heal and flourish. In addition, many of us have been praying that God would lead more persons of color to our church. We are seeking to become a more diverse community, to effectively reach the growing number of people from a range of ethnicities and races who live close to our church. Char's music ministry is an important signal to people of color that they are welcome, that they have a place, that they are represented.

Char ministers with such heart and soul—listeners are brought into God's presence by her humility and passion. She serves with increasing confidence and freedom and loves serving so much that we have to help her avoid burnout! When I watch her sing, I praise God for rescuing her and her family from leaving the faith and for blessing us with their presence and gifts.

RANDY'S STORY

Randy was a Steven Spielberg-type kid—already making movies with an 8-mm camera in junior high. His cutting-edge high school offered opportunities for students to hone their video skills by working for a local cable television station. Randy gradually discovered that his energy flowed most toward telling stories through images. But Randy rarely dared to dream he could ever make his living with such creative pursuits. While attending college in the Chicago area, Randy volunteered to help us edit videos on the night shift. It wasn't long before we recognized his gifts and enthusiasm and asked him to join our team.

Randy wins the prize for being the tallest member of our staff. At a notch under seven feet, he can just fit his legs under our video editing consoles. Randy provides leadership in our video department, using that art form to tell the stories he most wants to tell—stories of life change. He can't believe God granted him such a privilege. And we think Randy has only begun to scratch the surface of what God has called him to do. In the many years we hope he has ahead of him, imagine what stories are left to tell, what beautiful images he can assemble, how he will move us with his craft. I love how God made Randy.

GINA'S STORY

Gina was raised in an Italian-Catholic home and began a lifelong love affair with the violin at the age of nine. With single-minded passion, Gina aimed to become a professional concert violinist. In high school, Gina gave her life to Christ, partly as a result of our student ministry. For several years, Gina played her violin in a local symphony while simultaneously serving in our orchestra. She gradually discerned that while the music she played outside of church was sometimes more technically challenging, playing her notes for ministry was the only thing that stirred her soul. Gina says playing music at church has "brought life to my whole being."

These days Gina still performs at weddings and leads a string trio for other social events. But her deepest joy stems from the weeks our orchestra plays in mid-week worship services. Gina adds, "The people I serve and the purpose behind my performance make all the difference." This vibrant mother of three still practices seven to ten hours a week, developing her skills for the God who gave her the gift. She also provides leadership, encouragement, and inspiration for many other orchestra musicians.

Your church's scrapbook contains faces of people with stories just as powerful as those of Brian, Rhonda, Char, Randy, and Gina. Each face represents a life God called to faith and then launched into the spectacular adventure of using their gifts for almighty purposes. Some scrapbook pages in your book and mine are still empty, waiting to be filled with the faces of artists who are hesitant to step out of the shadows. They wait for an extended hand to draw them out, maybe just one *ask* away from joining in the ride of a lifetime.

Deep Personal Fulfillment

In addition to the unexpected gifts of seeing transformed lives and the joy of inviting artists to get in the game, I never expected to receive such intense personal fulfillment. I must first acknowledge that like most people I know in arts ministry, I've had moments—and sometimes even longer periods of time—when my ministry frustrations and disappointments triggered a "Who needs this?" cry in my soul. I look over the values I've described in this book and know that, truthfully, we are weak in more than one of them at any given time. Rarely does a church feel it is fully cranking on its vision, leading and developing the volunteers with tremendous care, and consistently crafting excellent, creative, authentic, transcendent weekly services all at the same time. At least that level of achievement hasn't been true for me and our team. And yet, most of the time, I drive toward church with a sense of great anticipation and privilege, even after three decades of ministry.

As we closed our weekly evaluation—after a weekend when God used our team beyond our expectations—one guy quietly said, "I can't believe we get to do this." We all looked at one another, silently acknowledging the profound truth our brother had given words to. Yes, it's hard—harder than most of us ever anticipated. But when we pause to recognize the wonder of what God allows us to do, it takes our breath away. God has given me the privilege for most of my adult life to spend the very best hours of my day doing what I believe I was born to do. I get to be creative—every day! I get to serve alongside people I deeply love, doing the most significant work of all—advancing the kingdom of God life by life. How could I have ever thought this path might be second best? For too long I allowed what the world considers most important for artists to influence my own sense of worth and significance. Finally, I know better.

If the almighty Creator has called you to serve the church with artistic or teaching gifts, you have the very highest of callings. I long for you to know, down to your toes, that you are not less than for making this choice. You are not **less than** those who record secular music or work for broadcast television or do live theater or make movies. On the contrary, you are a member of a team God is assembling to bring hope to the world through his Bride, the church. For the sake of people far from God, for artists in your local community, and yes, even for your own sake, I challenge you to fulfill your calling, to finish the race God has called you to. Run with every fiber of your being, with all your heart and soul and mind and strength. Together we create a legacy for the coming generations.

Church in Our Basement

If my daughters are alone in the basement, quiet for a few hours and not erupting in any big fights, my husband and I suspect they must be creating yet another production for us to enjoy. Some of their musicals, dances, and plays feature just the two of them; others include a friend. I truly can't count how many elaborate experiences they have crafted for an audience of two—many of which we've captured for all time on video to humiliate them someday. One evening we went out to dinner, leaving them with an older girl. When we returned, they announced that the three of them had prepared something new—not a play or musical. They had created a church service.

"This ought to be interesting," I commented to Warren, as we walked down to the basement and were handed a church "program." We took our seats, wondering just what these three young ladies had designed. Their printed programs were clean and simple, with a service title at the top. In the next few moments, we observed music, dance, and a dramatic sketch, all illustrating their main theme. My older daughter gave a brief teaching from the Bible. Afterward, they invited us upstairs for a post-church snack, just like many Willow attenders do when they eat together with friends in the church atrium. The girls were enthusiastic about their "church service" and couldn't wait for our reactions. Of course, we were delighted. It wasn't until later that I reflected more deeply on the meaning of that experience.

My daughters have grown up thinking it is normal for church to be fun, creative, excellent, and relevant. They can't imagine being bored on a Sunday morning or participating in a service that feels disconnected or unintentional. While they couldn't put words to it, they also expect people who sing, teach, and act to be real. Inauthenticity would seem strange to their little minds and hearts. And in their own childlike way, they did try to craft a sense of moment, hoping that people would be different in some way after the church experience. All these values are normal to them.

My passion is for every generation that follows mine to believe that church will be more than worth their time, that it truly will be compelling, relevant, authentic, creative, and excellent. This would be nothing short of a revolution. It can happen only if artists and teaching pastors in churches all over the world surrender lives and gifts to God, seeking to live out the values he calls us to embrace as we prepare the hour on Sunday.

Frederick Buechner describes *calling* as "the place where your deep gladness and the world's deep hunger meet." The world is ravenously hungry for a relationship with God—and many of us are deeply glad when we use our art to communicate truth. What a stunning combination.

I challenge you to be ruthlessly intentional, to lead and build a loving community of artists, to craft your services with all the excellence, creativity, and authenticity you can muster as you seek the anointing power of God in moments of transcendence, wonder, and transformation.

Together we can do this. And along the way you will discover, as I have, more joy and adventure than you can imagine.

AN HOUR ON SUNDAY BOOKMARK:

1-photocopy this page **2**-cut out the bookmark **3**-punch a hole at the top **4**-thread the hole with rafia, string or ribbon.

Father, may artists in local churches all over the planet follow your call and join the adventure of unleashing the arts for your purposes. May we dedicate ourselves to the creation of hours on Sunday that will have lasting impact, empowered by your Spirit to transform lives. Thank you for the awesome privilege of knowing we were born for this.

Go ahead and copy! Permission is hereby granted to reproduce this page.

aaAnd...that's a wrap!
GREAT job everybody.
now roll credits!

Credits

Just a fancy word for endNotes

1. **The Wonder of Sundays**

27   Garrison Keillor, as quoted by Ken Gire, *Windows of the Soul: Experiencing God in New Ways* (Grand Rapids: Zondervan, 1996), 120.

28   Ken Gire, *Windows of the Soul: Experiencing God in New Ways* (Grand Rapids: Zondervan, 1996), 16.

28   C.S. Lewis. After searching high and low, I was unable to find the original source for this quote. If you come across it, please let me know!

28   Elizabeth Barrett Browning, Oxford World's Classics Series, from *Aurora Leigh*, Book Seven, (Oxford: Oxford University Press, 1998), lines 821-825.

28   Frederick Buechner, *Telling the Truth: The Gospel as Tragedy, Comedy, and Fairy Tale* (San Francisco: HarperSanFrancisco, 1977), 44.

29   George Bernard Shaw, as quoted by Gire, *Windows of the Soul*, 41.

29   Thornton Wilder, *Our Town* (New York: HarperCollins, 1998), 108.

30   Aleksander Solzhenitsyn, from his "Nobel Lecture on Literature," as quoted by Gire, *Windows of the Soul*, 121.

2. Intentionality, Part 1

No notes.

3. Intentionality, Part 2

No notes.

4. Leadership

76   Anne Lamott, *Bird by Bird: Some Instructions on Writing and Life* (New York: Anchor, 1995), 6.

77   Warren Bennis and Patricia Ward Biederman, *Organizing Genius: The Secrets of Creative Collaboration* (New York: Basic Books, 1998), 54.

80   Gordon MacKenzie, *Orbiting the Giant Hairball: A Corporate Fool's Guide to Surviving with Grace* (New York: Viking Press, 1998), 63.

5. Community

No notes.

6. Evaluation

110   Parker J. Palmer, *Let Your Life Speak: Listening for the Voice of Vocation* (San Francisco: Jossey-Bass Publishers, 1999), 87.

7. Well-ordered Hearts and Lives

134   David Halberstam, *Playing for Keeps: Michael Jordan and the World He Made* (New York: Random House, 1999), 12, 14.

still rolling...

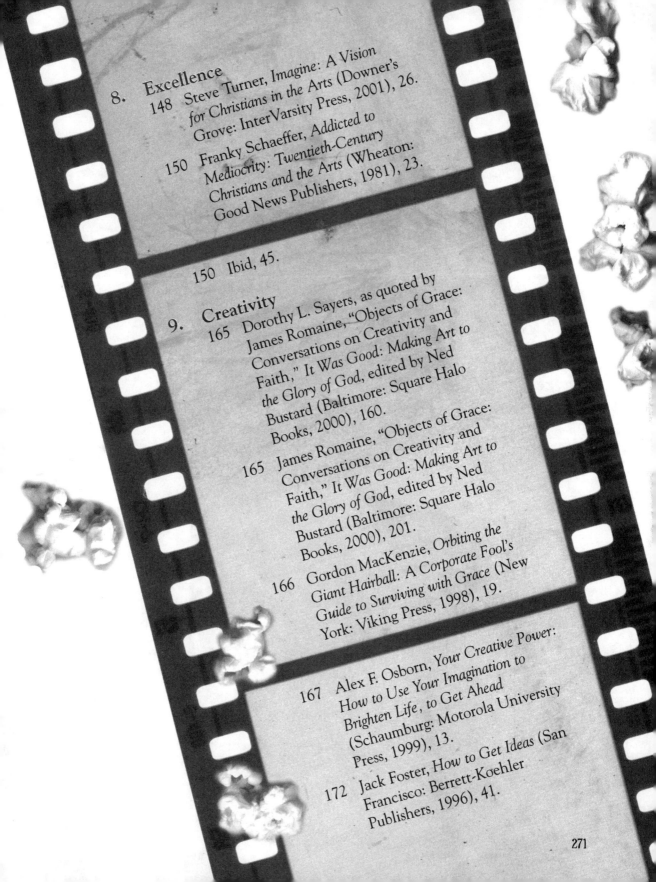

8. **Excellence**

148 Steve Turner, *Imagine: A Vision for Christians in the Arts* (Downer's Grove: InterVarsity Press, 2001), 26.

150 Franky Schaeffer, *Addicted to Mediocrity: Twentieth-Century Christians and the Arts* (Wheaton: Good News Publishers, 1981), 23.

150 Ibid, 45.

9. **Creativity**

165 Dorothy L. Sayers, as quoted by James Romaine, "Objects of Grace: Conversations on Creativity and Faith," *It Was Good: Making Art to the Glory of God*, edited by Ned Bustard (Baltimore: Square Halo Books, 2000), 160.

165 James Romaine, "Objects of Grace: Conversations on Creativity and Faith," *It Was Good: Making Art to the Glory of God*, edited by Ned Bustard (Baltimore: Square Halo Books, 2000), 201.

166 Gordon MacKenzie, *Orbiting the Giant Hairball: A Corporate Fool's Guide to Surviving with Grace* (New York: Viking Press, 1998), 19.

167 Alex F. Osborn, *Your Creative Power: How to Use Your Imagination to Brighten Life, to Get Ahead* (Schaumburg: Motorola University Press, 1999), 13.

172 Jack Foster, *How to Get Ideas* (San Francisco: Berrett-Koehler Publishers, 1996), 41.

174 Anne Lamott, *Bird by Bird: Some Instructions on Writing and Life* (New York: Anchor, 1995), 99.

175 Louis Pasteur, as quoted by Richard Florida, *The Rise of the Creative Class: And How It's Transforming Work, Leisure, Community and Everyday Life* (New York: Basic Books, 2002), 34.

176 Gordon MacKenzie, *Orbiting the Giant Hairball*, 216.

176 David Ogilvy, as quoted by Florida, *The Rise of the Creative Class*, 21.

178 Roger von Oech, *A Whack on the Side of the Head: How You Can Be More Creative*, Revised Edition (New York: Warner Books, 1998), 101.

180 Jeffrey Pfeffer, as quoted by Florida, *The Rise of the Creative Class*, 141.

180 Richard Florida, *The Rise of the Creative Class*, 131.

182 Jack Foster, *How to Get Ideas* (San Francisco: Berrett-Koehler Publishers, 1996), 90.

10. Authenticity

186 Walter Kirn, "What Would Jesus Do?," GQ Magazine, September 2002, 496.

191 Emory A. Griffin, *The Mind Changers: The Art of Christian Persuasion* (Wheaton: Tyndale House Publishers, 1976), 116.

193 J. Keith Miller, *A Hunger for Healing: The Twelve Steps as a Classic Model for Spiritual Growth* (San Francisco: HarperSanFrancisco, 1991), 116.

"STICKY" POPCORN

INGREDIENTS:
2 QTS POPCORN
½ C White corn syrup
TWO sticks butter
1⅓ C Sugar

194 C.S. Lewis, "Christian Behavior," *The Best of C.S. Lewis* (Grand Rapids: Baker Book House, 1977), 502.

196 G.K. Chesterton, "A Defence of Humility," *The Defendant, Collected Works of G.K. Chesterton* (Classic Books, 2000).

196 Joseph M. Stowell, *Perilous Pursuits: Our Obsession with Significance* (Chicago: Moody Press, 1994), 145.

197 Dallas Willard, *The Divine Conspiracy: Rediscovering Our Hidden Life in God* (San Francisco: HarperSanFrancisco, 1998), 200.

11. **Transcendent Moments**
206 Frederick Buechner, *Now and Then: A Memoir of Vocation* (San Francisco: HarperSanFrancisco, 1983), 87.

12. **Transformational Teaching**
240 Frederick Buechner, *Telling the Truth: The Gospel as Tragedy, Comedy and Fairy Tale* (San Francisco: HarperSanFrancisco, 1977), 40.

13. **The Rewards of Sundays**
264 Frederick Buechner, *Wishful Thinking: A Theological ABC* (San Francisco HarperSanFrancisco, 1973), 95.

DirecTioNs: POP the corn. COMBiNe all the Other stuff in a saucePAN. COoK uNtil StRiNgy.

put POPPed corn On a COOKie tray that's LiNed with wAx PaPER. POUr sticky goo Over popcOrn. Let COOL AND EAt !

Willow Creek Association
vision, training, resources, for prevailing churches

This resource was created to serve you and to help you build a local church that prevails. It is just one of many ministry tools that are part of the Willow Creek Resources® line, published by the Willow Creek Association together with Zondervan.

The Willow Creek Association (WCA) was created in 1992 to serve a rapidly growing number of churches from across the denominational spectrum that are committed to helping unchurched people become fully devoted followers of Christ. Membership in the WCA now numbers over 10,000 Member Churches worldwide from more than ninety denominations.

The Willow Creek Association links like-minded Christian leaders with each other and with strategic vision, training and resources in order to help them build prevailing churches designed to reach their redemptive potential. Here are some of the ways the WCA does that.

- **Prevailing Church Conference**—an annual two-day event, held at Willow Creek Community Church in South Barrington, Illinois, to help pioneering church leaders raise up a volunteer core while discovering new and innovative ways to build prevailing churches that reach unchurched people.

- **The Leadership Summit**—a once-a-year, two-and-a-half-day conference to envision and equip Christians with leadership gifts and responsibilities. Presented live at Willow Creek as well as via satellite broadcast to over eighty locations across North America, this event is designed to increase the leadership effectiveness of pastors, ministry staff, volunteer church leaders and Christians in the marketplace.

- **Ministry-Specific Conferences**—throughout each year the WCA hosts a variety of conferences and training events—both at Willow Creek's main campus and offsite, across the U.S. and around the world—targeting church leaders in ministry-specific areas such as: evangelism, the arts, children, students, small groups, preaching and teaching, spiritual formation, spiritual gifts, raising up resources, etc.

- **Willow Creek Resources®**—to provide churches with trusted and field-tested ministry resources in such areas as leadership, evangelism, spiritual formation, spiritual gifts, small groups, stewardship, student ministry, children's ministry, the use of the arts—drama, media, contemporary music—and more. For additional information about Willow Creek Resources® call the Customer Service Center at 800-570-9812. Outside the U.S. call 847-765-0070.

 WillowNet—the WCA's Internet resource service, which provides access to hundreds of transcripts of Willow Creek messages, drama scripts, songs, videos and multimedia tools. The system allows users to sort through these elements and download them for a fee. Visit us online at www.willowcreek.com.

 WCA News—a quarterly publication to inform you of the latest trends, resources and information on WCA events from around the world.

 Defining Moments—a monthly audio journal for church leaders featuring Bill Hybels and other Christian leaders discussing probing issues to help you discover biblical principles and transferable strategies to maximize your church's redemptive potential.

 The Exchange—our online classified ads service to assist churches in recruiting key staff for ministry positions.

Member Benefits—includes substantial discounts to WCA training events, a 20 percent discount on all Willow Creek Resources®, access to a Members-Only section on WillowNet, monthly communications, and more. Member Churches also receive special discounts and premier services through WCA's growing number of Select Service Providers and Preferred Ministry Partners.

For specific information about WCA membership, upcoming conferences and other ministry services contact:

WILLOW CREEK ASSOCIATION
P.O. BOX 3188, Barrington, IL 60011-3188
Phone: 847-570-9812 Fax: 847-765-5046
www.willowcreek.com

The Willow Creek Arts Conference

What can happen in an hour on Sunday?

Come see for yourself. When artists and leaders in the church come together, the results are compelling.

assumptions changed.

Lives Touched.

eternities redirected.

The annual Willow Creek Arts Conference. A one-of-a-kind gathering, designed especially for artists and leaders who, together, use their gifts to craft that all-important hour on Sunday—a powerful, relevant church service filled with transformational moments that open the hearts of both believers and seekers to God.

Bring your entire team and you will . . .

- Discover why the arts are crucial to the mission of your church.
- Find new ways to express your art to advance the cause of Christ.
- Sit back and laugh, cry, sing, worship and enjoy being on the receiving end of a year's worth of new dramas, music, production and teaching from the Willow Creek arts team.
- Choose from more than seventy hands-on breakout sessions.
- Network with other Christian artists and church teams.
- Allow us to minister to you, so you can return home creatively and spiritually recharged, ready to recommit your gifts and talents to advancing the important work of your prevailing church.

Join us for the Willow Creek
Arts Conference this June!
for more information,
visit www.willowcreek.com
or call 847.765.0070.

a special gift for
you! A place to...

JOurNaL

take notes

write songs,
        Poetry

stick your gum

sketch
dOodle
etc...etc...etc...

Okay, this is really the end. . . you can shut your book now!

We want to hear from you. Please send your comments about this book to us in care of zreview@zondervan.com. Thank you.

ZONDERVAN™

GRAND RAPIDS, MICHIGAN 49530 USA

WWW.ZONDERVAN.COM